THE TOTAL ROCK DRUMMER

>> A Fun and Comprehensive Overview of Rock Drumming

MIKE MICHALKOW

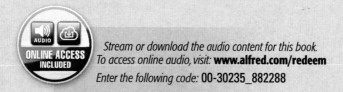

Stream or download the audio content for this book.
To access online audio, visit: **www.alfred.com/redeem**
Enter the following code: 00-30235_882288

Alfred Music
P.O. Box 10003
Van Nuys, CA 91410-0003
alfred.com

ISBN-10: 0-7390-5268-3 (Book & Online Audio)
ISBN-13: 978-0-7390-5268-6 (Book & Online Audio)

Cover photography © Photodisc / Alamy
Drumset on cover courtesy CB Educational Percussion / Kaman Music Corporation

Audio recorded by Brent Ellis at LS Records Studio, Abbotsford, B.C., Canada
Mixed and mastered by Mark Schane-Lydon at WorkshopLive.com, Pittsfield, MA

Table of Contents

About the Author

Mike Michalkow hails from Winnipeg, Canada and has been drumming since the age of 17. He maintains a busy teaching, performance, and recording schedule, covering a range of styles, including progressive rock, Latin, jazz, blues, pop, folk, Celtic, country, metal, and R&B. His current rock project is playing with R30: A Tribute to Rush.

Mike plays and endorses Yamaha drums, Evans drumheads, Sabian cymbals, Vic Firth drumsticks, Hansenfutz accessory pedals, Blow It Fans, and LP percussion. He is also a clinician for Yamaha drums on the full acoustic and electronic line.

Mike is the author of an instructional DVD, *The Moeller Method Series*, and two training packs (DVD, book, and play-along CD) entitled *The Jazz Drumming System* and *The Latin Drumming System*.

Since 2000, Mike has been head of the west coast drum department (Los Angeles, San Francisco, and Seattle) for the National Guitar Workshop.

For more about the author, please visit: www.mikemichalkow.com.

PHOTO BY BOB FUGGER

Acknowledgements

Thanks to the following people: My wife, Tracy; my mother, Kay; my brother, Randy; my cousin, Gerry Trach; and the rest of my supportive family. David Smolover, Nat Gunod, Burgess Speed, Timothy Phelps, Mark "Monk" Schane-Lydon, and the rest of the staff at Workshop Arts, thank you for making this happen! Steven Novacek, Gayle Novacek, and Nate Jarrell from the National Guitar Workshop west coast campuses. Ken Infanti, Sean Browne, and Larry Mansbridge at Yamaha Music Canada. Robert Mason and Ann McNally at Sabian Cymbals Canada. Neil Larivee and Scott Atkins at Vic Firth drumsticks. Mark Cubranich and the staff at Hansenfutz. Larry Davidson at Evans Drumheads Canada. James Abell at Blow It Fans. Brent Ellis from LS Records. Kevin Hughes, my Seattle buddy who always forces me to ROCK! Michael Burley and Gord Esau from R30: A Tribute to Rush—you guys push my limits and I love it!! All of my present and past students who continue to support and inspire me to be the best teacher I can be. All of the great drummers mentioned throughout this book, thank you for the inspiration. Thank you for purchasing this book, and may your rock drumming adventure be successful and fun.

This book is dedicated to the memory of my father, Alex Alfred Michalkow.

Introduction

Welcome to *The Total Rock Drummer*. This book and accompanying audio have been designed to help the beginner develop all the essential skills needed to be an advanced rock drummer in a short period of time. You will learn how to count and play all the important note values in rock drumming as well as develop all the essential beats, fills, and concepts employed by today's rock drummers.

In order to begin learning a new style of music or drumming, you must listen to the music as much as possible. Obtain as many rock albums as you can, check out live rock bands, and watch concerts on DVD.

It is also very important to study with a good teacher. Drummers who are self-taught never really know if they are doing things correctly. Remember, the more you know, the better you become, and your chances of becoming a paid professional drummer are much higher.

Be patient—some exercises may come easier than others—stay focused, practice hard, and have fun!

Suggestions for Using This Book

- Once you've worked through the chapters of this book, try going back to the exercises from time to time to see if you can play them faster and with more precision.

- Practice with a *metronome*, an electronic timekeeping device that generates a "click" at the tempo of your choice.

- Practice with various *dynamics* (volume levels), from loud to soft.

- Get creative with some of the beats and fills that are demonstrated in the book by combining them in interesting patterns and developing your own variations.

- Use the accompanying audio to hear how certain exercises are played.

Track 0

A

Companion audio is included with this book. Using the audio will help make learning more enjoyable and the information more meaningful. Listening to the recording will help you correctly interpret the rhythms and feel of each example. The icon at the top left appears next to each example performed in the recording. The track number corresponds directly to the example you want to hear. Many of the examples are divided into multiple variations, indicated with a letter (A, B, C, etc.). If the variation is included in the audio, it will be indicated with a smaller version of the icon above the corresponding variation (bottom left). Enjoy!

Chapter 1: Getting Started

Parts of the Drumset

The image below shows a typical drumset. The components include snare drum (1), tom toms (2), floor tom (3), bass drum (4), hi-hat (5), crash cymbal (6), and ride cymbal (7).

A Note for Left-Handed Drummers

This book is written from the point of view of a right-handed drummer. If you are a left-handed drummer, your drumset may be a mirror image of the right-handed kit shown above. As you work through the book, simply reverse any mention of left and right hands. For example, if instructed to play the sticking "RRLR," you would play "LLRL" instead.

Holding the Drumsticks

The following steps will teach you to hold the drumsticks comfortably and correctly.

Step 1. Hold out your hand as if you were going to shake someone's hand.

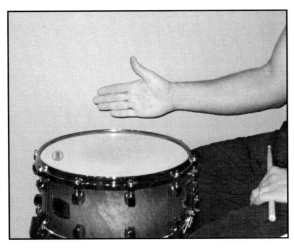

Step 2. Make a "gun" with your index finger and thumb.

Step 3. Point your index finger towards the center of the snare drum.

Step 4. Lay your hand down just above the snare drum, palm facing up.

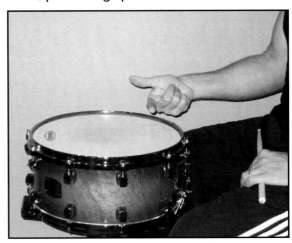

Step 5. Place the drumstick inside the first joint of your index finger and locate the balance point (the point where the stick will naturally rebound).

Step 6. Secure the stick by placing your thumb on top of the drumstick, creating the fulcrum.

Step 7. Turn your hand over so that your palm is facing downward.

Step 8. Lift the drumstick off of the drum so that it is pointing straight up.

Step 9. Gently secure your remaining fingers on the stick (do not grip too tightly).

Step 10. Repeat all the steps with the opposite hand. Once you've done that, rest the tips of the sticks at the center of the drum to create a 90-degree angle between the sticks.

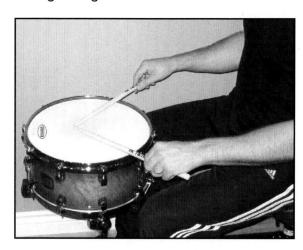

Chapter 2: Basic Notation and Theory

Drumset Notational Key

The following notational key shows you how each drum or cymbal is notated on the musical *staff*. The staff consists of five lines, and each line or space corresponds to a specific drum or cymbal. A *percussion clef* at the beginning of the staff indicates the music is written for drums, as opposed to some other instrument.

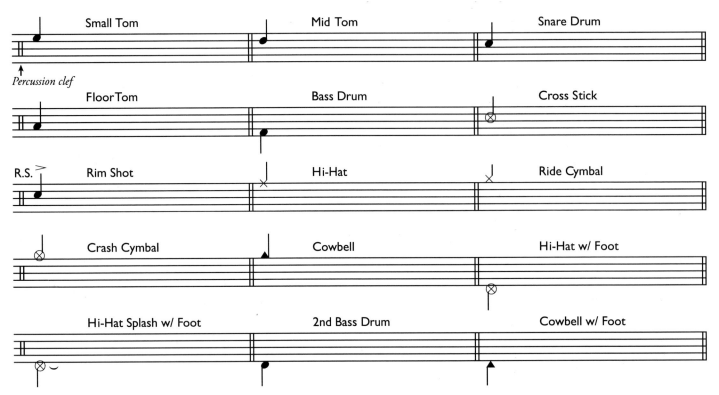

Try to memorize this key. In the beginning, you may need to refer back to this page if you are uncertain of where a drum or cymbal is placed on the staff.

Notes and Rests

Notes and *rests* form the rhythmic "alphabet" of music. Notes indicate sound, and rests indicate silence. You need to memorize the shape and appearance of these notes and rests and be able to quickly identify them on the staff before you can learn how to count them or begin using them in musical contexts. Below are the symbols that indicate the different types of notes and rests.

Notes—Duration of Sound

Rests—Duration of Silence

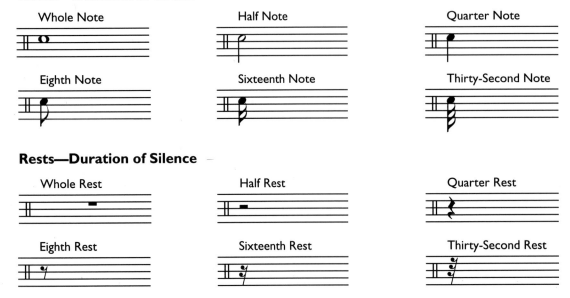

Note Value Chart

The following chart introduces the "alphabet" of rhythm and teaches you how to count musical notes. This book will cover all of these rhythms through the various exercises. Each chapter will focus on one or more of these note values (the term "value" refers to the length or duration of a note), so refer back to this page periodically to learn how to count each type of note properly.

Track 1

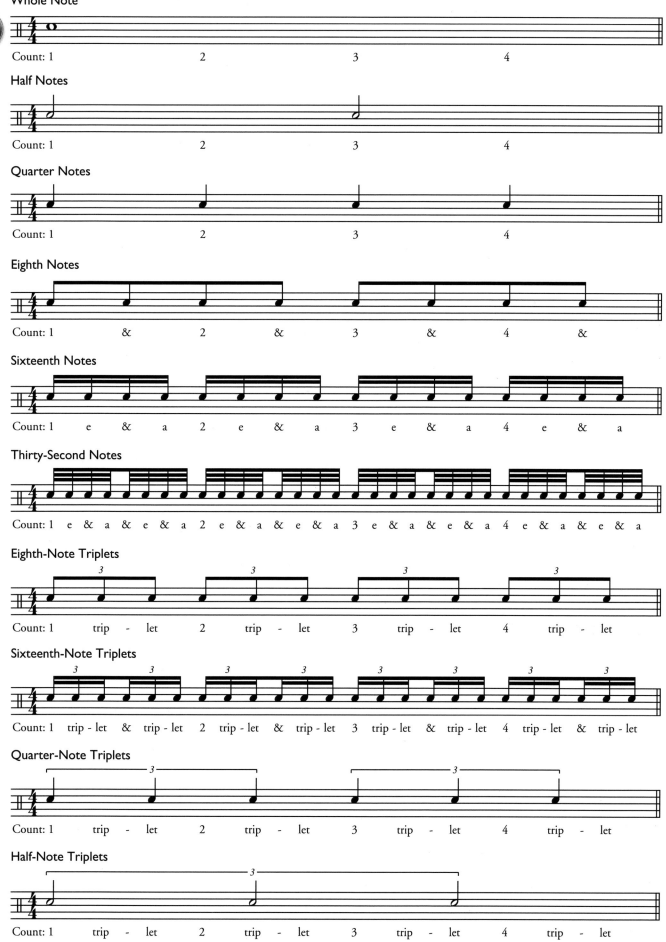

Time Signatures

The *time* or *meter* of a piece is indicated by two numbers placed at the beginning of the staff, one on top of the other. This is called the *time signature*.

The upper number indicates how many beats are to be played per measure. The lower number tells us the note value that receives the beat. For example:

4 = Four beats to the measure
4 = Quarter note receives one beat

7 = Seven beats to the measure
8 = Eighth note receives one beat

Dynamics

Dynamics is the musical term for changes in volume. In this section, you will learn the terms for various volumes, whether soft, loud, very loud, etc. The bold letters in parentheses are the symbols used in standard drum notation to indicate which dynamic you must play.

Piano (***p***) = Soft

Pianissimo (***pp***) = Very soft

Pianississimo (***ppp***) = Very, very soft

Mezzo Piano (***mp***) = Moderately soft

Forte (***f***) = Loud

Fortissimo (***ff***) = Very loud

Fortississimo (***fff***) = Very, very loud

Mezzo Forte (***mf***) = Moderately loud

Forte Piano (***fp***) = Accent strongly, diminishing instantly to piano

Crescendo (⟨————⟩) = Gradually louder

Decrescendo (⟩————⟨) = Gradually softer

Accent (>) = Play the accented note louder than the notes around it

Different Notation Styles

There are different notation styles used in this book. In any particular instance, the style that is used is the one that best represents the musical idea at the time.

In the example below, the stems of the snare drum go up and the bass drum go down. This provides some visual separation of the hands and feet.

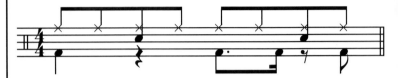

In the next example, the hi-hat stems are written going up and the bass and snare are going down.

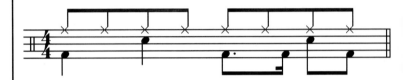

You may also see all of the stems going up, as in the example below.

Whole Notes, Half Notes, and Quarter Notes

In the following exercises, we'll explore how to count and play whole notes, half notes, and quarter notes. We'll also look at the corresponding rests for each of these note values. Be sure to always count to four for all of these exercises, since they all use the $\frac{4}{4}$ time signature.

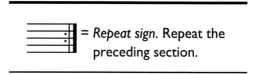
= *Repeat sign.* Repeat the preceding section.

Whole Notes

A whole note receives four beats (the whole measure). Strike the snare drum on beat 1 and let the sound ring out for the duration of four beats.

Whole Rests

A whole rest indicates four beats of silence. (When counting numbers appear in musical examples in this book, parentheses are used to indicate rests.)

Half Notes

A half note receives two beats (half of the measure in $\frac{4}{4}$).

Half Rests

A half rest indicates two beats of silence. Play the half note on beat 1, which will last two beats, then rest on beats 3 and 4.

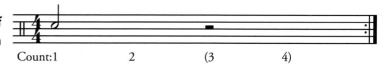

Quarter Notes

Quarter notes are the essential beats in many types of music. The quarter note is also referred to as *the beat* or *the pulse*. The quarter note receives one beat. There are four quarter notes in a measure of $\frac{4}{4}$.

Quarter Rests

A quarter rest indicates silence for one beat. In this example, we play beat 1, rest on beat 2, play beat 3, and rest on beat 4.

Quarter-Note Exercise

In the following exercise, be sure to count all four quarter notes (or rests) aloud. If you have a metronome, start slowly and keep the pace steady and even.

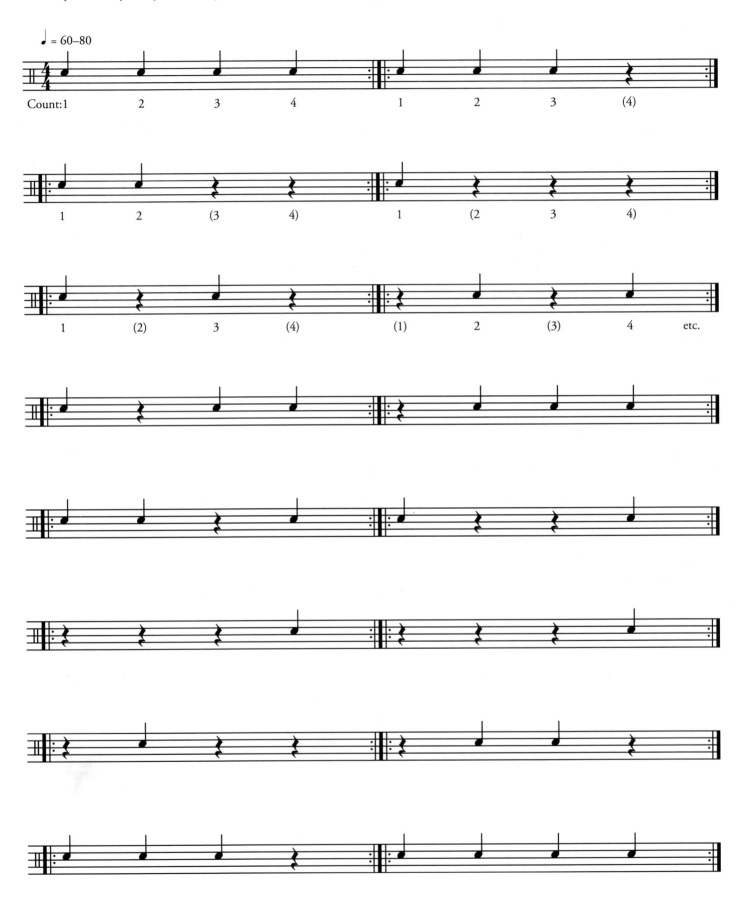

Whole-, Half-, and Quarter-Note Exercise

This exercise combines whole notes, half notes, quarter notes, and their corresponding rests. Make sure you count aloud when first attempting this exercise. Take it one measure at a time. The goal is to play the entire exercise without stopping.

♩ = 60–80

Count: 1   2   3   4   1   2   3   4   1   2   3   4   1   2   3   4 etc.

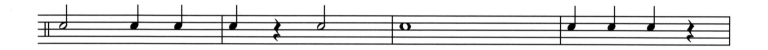

Constructing a Basic Beat Using Quarter Notes

Providing a *beat* can be defined as the drummer's "role" when performing with a band. A beat is what the drummer maintains throughout a song, usually while playing a cymbal, the snare drum, and the bass drum. In this exercise, you will learn how to construct a basic beat by separating each part (hi-hat, snare drum, bass drum) then combining them to create your first drum beat.

Track 2

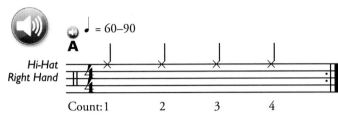

Finally, put all the parts together to play a *basic quarter-note beat*, also known as a *classic two beat*.

Four Basic Drum Rudiments

A *drum rudiment* is a basic building block of the drumming vocabulary, much like scales and chords for guitarists. As drummers, we use combinations of right- and left-hand sticking patterns to create drum fills, beats, and solos.

The following examples use lots of sixteenth notes (refer to page 9 if you need a reminder of how they are counted).

They can look intimidating on the page, but as a drummer, it's important to develop a strong internal sense of the sixteenth-note pulse. Listen carefully to the recording to get the sound in your head, and skip ahead to page 25 for a more detailed explanation.

R = Right hand
L = Left hand

Single-Stroke Roll

Double-Stroke Roll

The next rudiment, called the *paradiddle*, is a combination of single-stroke and double-stroke rolls.

Single Paradiddle

The next rudiment, called the *flam*, is performed by striking the drum with both sticks at almost the same time. The first stick hits an instant before the second stick and is notated as a *grace note* with no rhythmic value or "count" of its own.

♪ = Grace note

Flam

Track 3

Be certain to always practice your rudiments. Keep them consistent and clean. Over time, you'll be amazed at what you can do by incorporating them into your playing.

Chapter 3: Eighth Notes and Rests

There are eight "eighth" notes in a full bar of $\frac{4}{4}$ time.
Here's how they are counted:

Count: 1   &   2   &   3   &   4   &

The following examples show some of the possible combinations of eighth notes and eighth rests.

1   &   (2   &)   3   &   (4   &)

1   (&)   2   (&)   3   (&)   4   (&)

(1)   &   (2)   &   (3)   &   (4)   &

1   &   2   &   (3)   &   4   (&)

1   &   (2)   &   3   &   (4)   &

(1)   &   2   &   (3)   &   4   &

1   &   2   (&)   3   &   4   (&)

Eighth-Note Snare Drum Exercise

The following exercise should be practiced on the snare drum or a *practice pad* (a flat rubber surface for quiet practicing). It allows you to see how eighth notes are counted and played with various rests throughout the examples.

Count all of the eighth notes (1–&, 2–&, 3–&, 4–&) when practicing these. You will see these patterns more often as you proceed through this book. Once you've worked on each measure individually, try playing them all nonstop.

Count: 1 & 2 & 3 & 4 & 1 & 2 & 3 & 4 & etc.

Eighth-Note Rock Beats

Here are some of the most popular rock beats ever. Eighth-note beats are the norm in rock and popular music. Drummers who come to mind that use these beats in their playing are: Phil Rudd of AC/DC, John Bonham of Led Zeppelin, Stewart Copeland of the Police, Matt Sorum of Guns 'N' Roses/Velvet Revolver, Dave Grohl of Nirvana, Nick Mason of Pink Floyd, and Lars Ulrich of Metallica, just to name a few.

Eighth-Note Fills

A *drum fill* provides an opportunity for the drummer to deviate from the drum beat and venture around the drumset to set up a new section of a song. A fill can be played at the beginning of a song, at the end of a phrase, or to set up a new section of a song. Fills can be very short, very long, or somewhere in between. In the following examples, you will learn to play a one-bar fill using eighth notes. (On page 22, you will find some examples of how you can combine beats and fills.) Keep a close eye on the sticking patterns when provided.

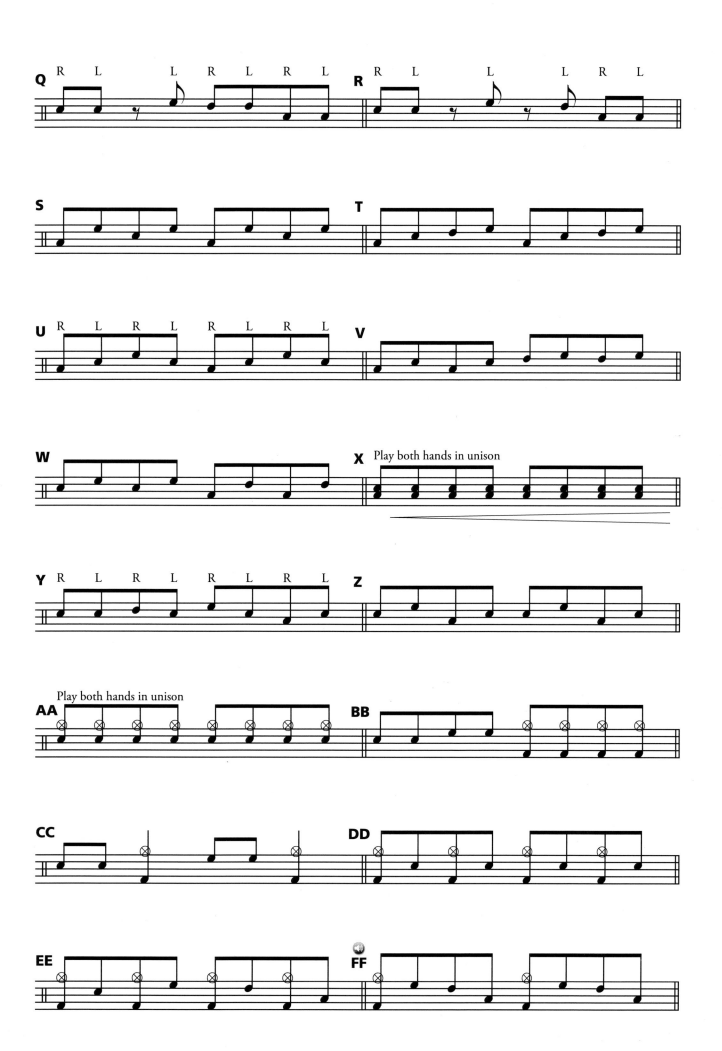

Eighth-Note Beat/Fill Combinations

The following exercises alternate between one-bar drum beats and fills. Practice slowly at first and work on speeding up the tempo.

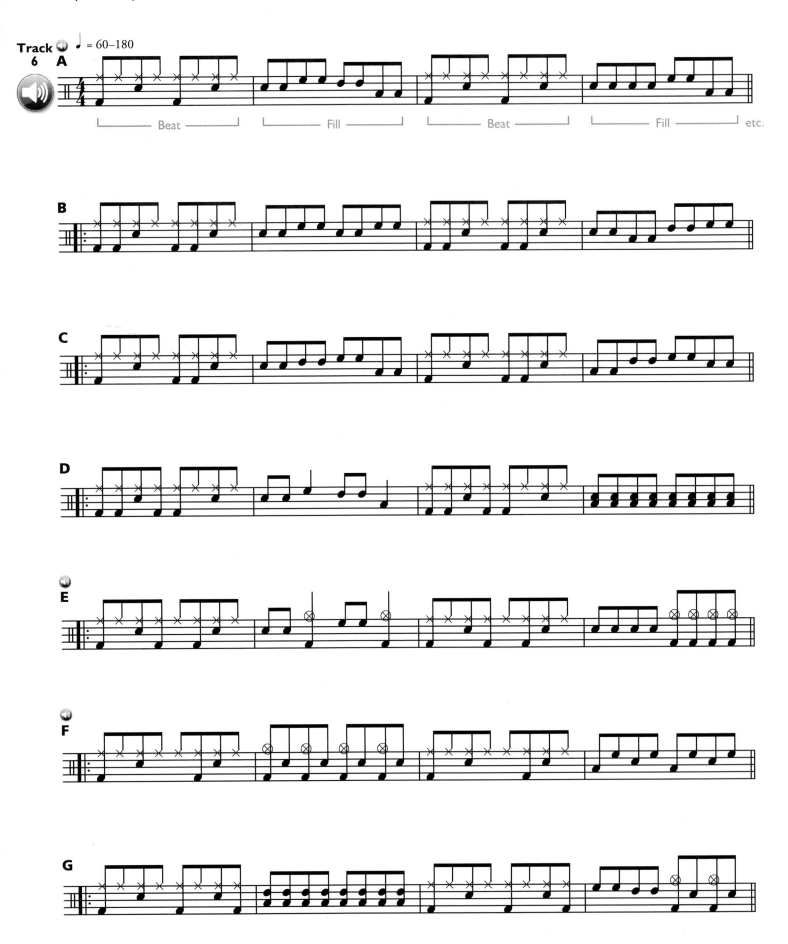

Eighth-Note Tom Tom Beats

Tom tom beats create a powerful low-end groove. You'll notice while practicing these beats that they sound quite a bit different than the beats you've already learned. Keep the eighth-note count happening throughout these exercises. Count aloud at first to make sure you are playing them correctly. Tom tom beats are very popular, especially in classic rock. Drummers like Ginger Baker of Cream and Ringo Starr of the Beatles used many of these beats in their music.

Add the bass drum to the following tom tom beats

Chapter 4: Sixteenth Notes and Rests

Sixteenth notes divide the quarter note into four equal parts. In other words, there are four sixteenth notes in one quarter note. Notice that groups of four sixteenth notes are joined together with a double beam.

Sixteenth notes are counted "1–e–&–a, 2–e–&–a, 3–e–&–a, 4–e–&–a."

Count: 1   e   &   a   2   e   &   a   3   e   &   a   4   e   &   a

In the following example, you will rest on the *onbeats* (1, 2, 3, 4) and play the "e–&–a."

Count: (1)   e   &   a   (2)   e   &   a   (3)   e   &   a   (4)   e   &   a

In the example below, you will play all the sixteenth notes, except for the onbeats 2 and 4.

Count: 1   e   &   a   (2)   e   &   a   3   e   &   a   (4)   e   &   a

In this example, you will rest on the "e" of each beat and play the remaining sixteenth notes.

Count: 1   (e)   &   a   2   (e)   &   a   3   (e)   &   a   4   (e)   &   a

Sixteenth-Note Snare Drum Exercises

The following exercise should be practiced on the snare drum or practice pad. It allows you to see how sixteenth notes are counted and played with various rests and quarter notes throughout the examples. Count all of the sixteenth notes (1–e–&–a, 2–e–&–a, 3–e–&–a, 4–e–&–a) when practicing these. You will begin to see these patterns more often as you proceed through this book. Once you've worked on each measure individually, try playing them all nonstop.

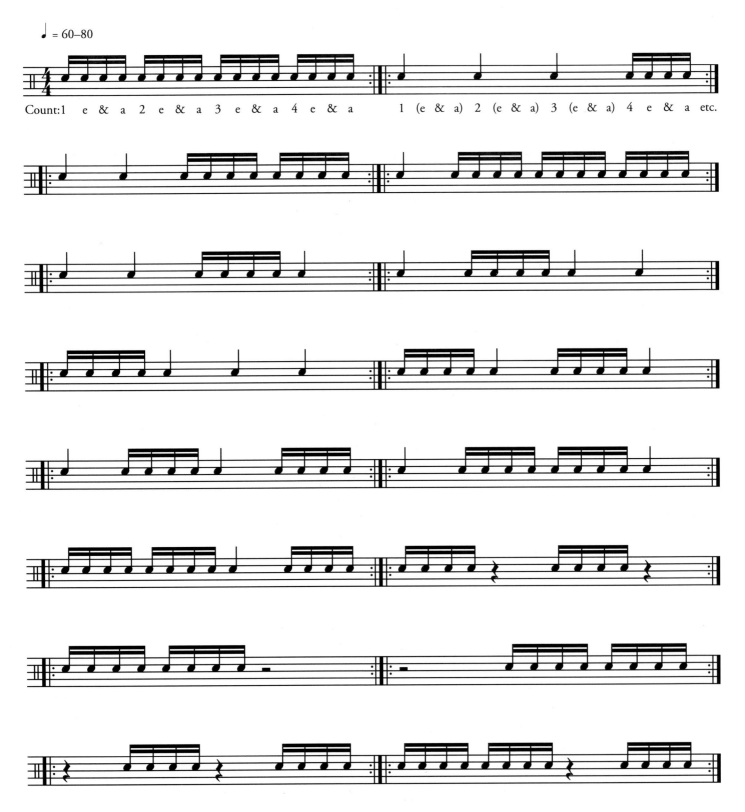

Combining Quarter Notes, Eighth Notes, and Sixteenth Notes

It's time to combine the three note values you've learned to create some cool rhythmic patterns. Practice these on a practice pad or snare drum. Be certain to count and use a metronome. Throughout the book, you will start to see how these combined rhythms make up fills and solos. Once you've practiced each measure separately, try playing them all nonstop.

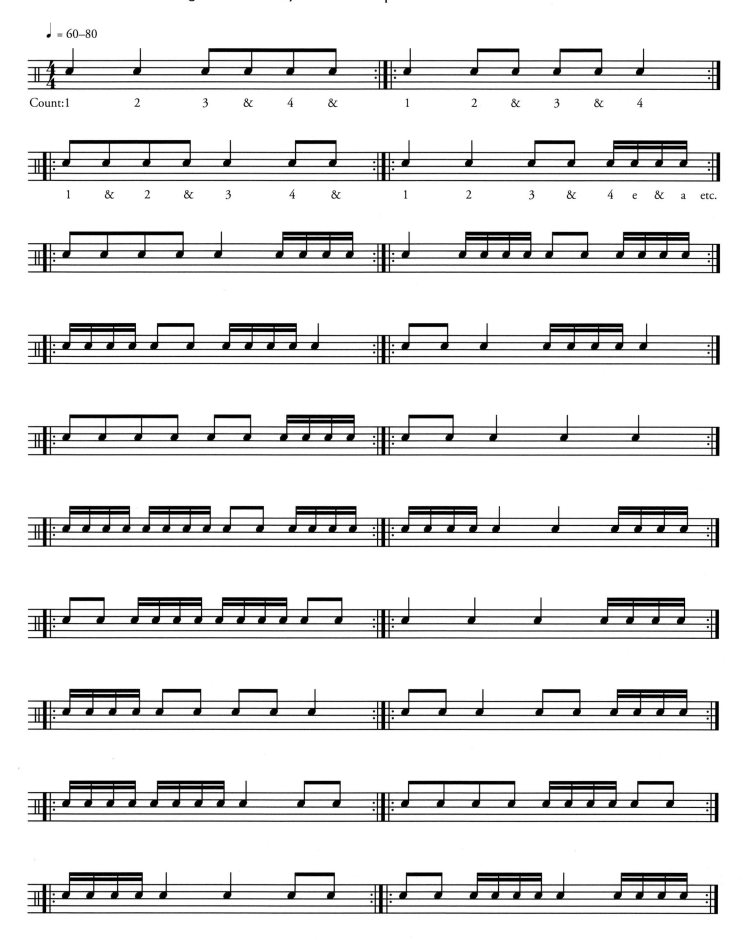

Sixteenth-Note Rock Beats

In these exercises, play all the sixteenth-notes on the hi-hat (all with the right hand) and play the snare drum on beats 2 and 4.

You'll notice that the bass drum pattern varies from exercise to exercise. Be sure to count sixteenth notes while practicing these.

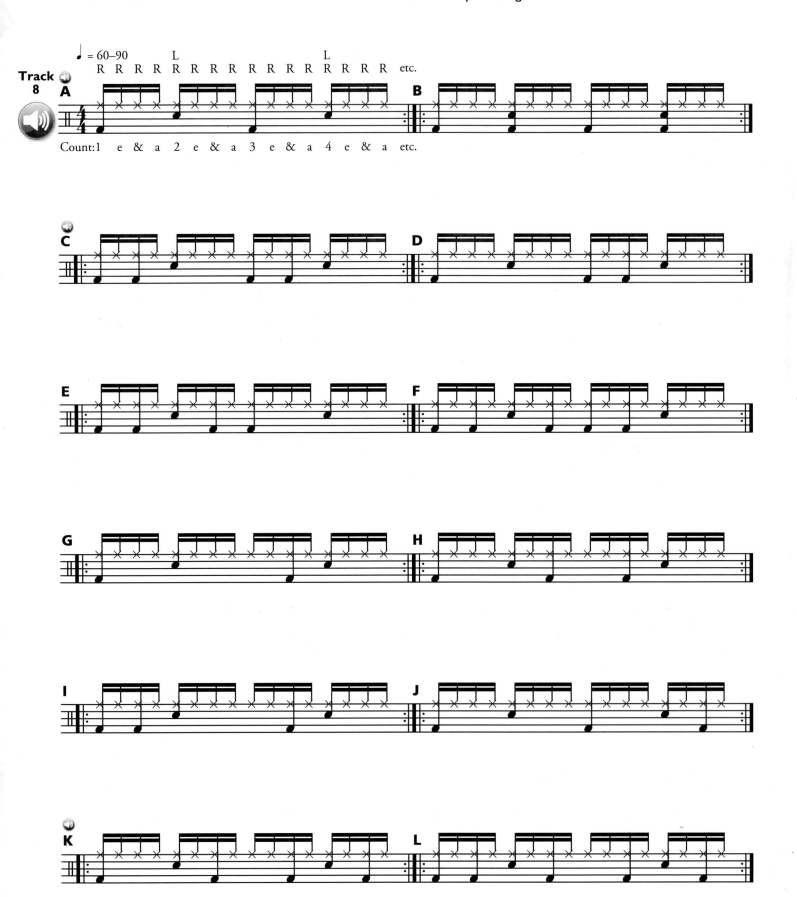

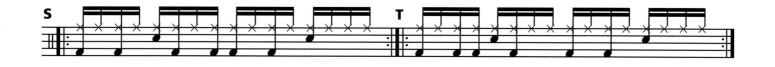

Sixteenth-Note Rock Fills

It's time to start learning sixteenth-note rock fills. Keep the sixteenth-note rhythm consistent throughout these exercises. Some of the fills add the bass drum to make things more interesting. Start slowly, be patient, and have fun!

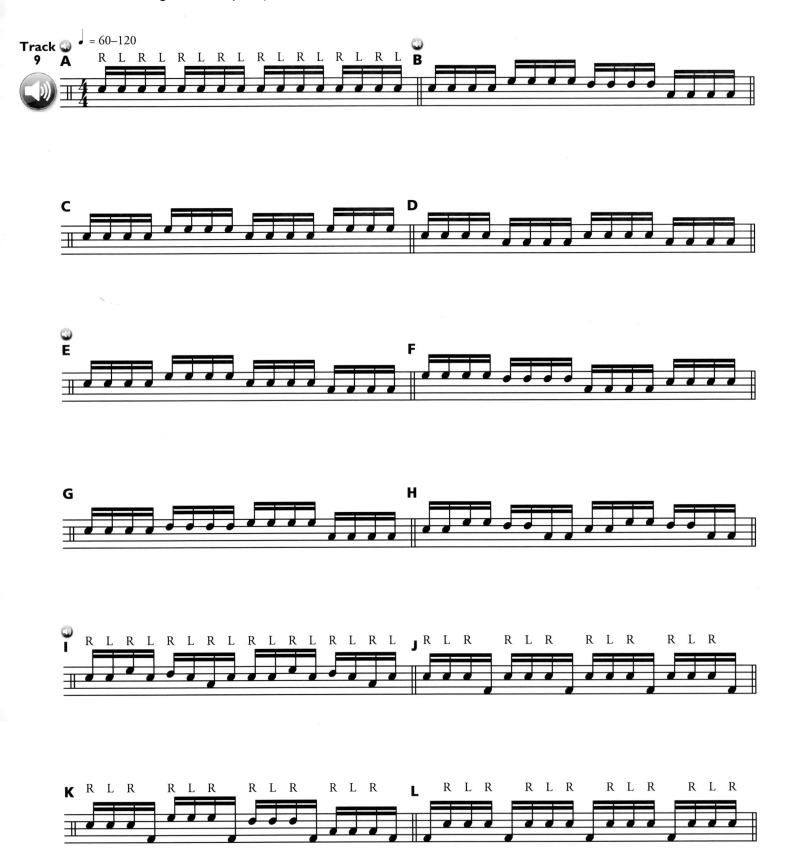

Sixteenth-Note Groupings

This page displays all the different groups of sixteenth-note rhythms using rests, dotted rests, and dotted notes. Start memorizing and understanding how these rhythms look and are played. You will begin to see these rhythms throughout the book in fills, cymbal patterns, bass drum beats, and more.

A *dot* placed after a note or rest increases its duration by one half of its original value. For example, a dotted eighth note equals an eighth plus a sixteenth note.

♪. = Dotted note

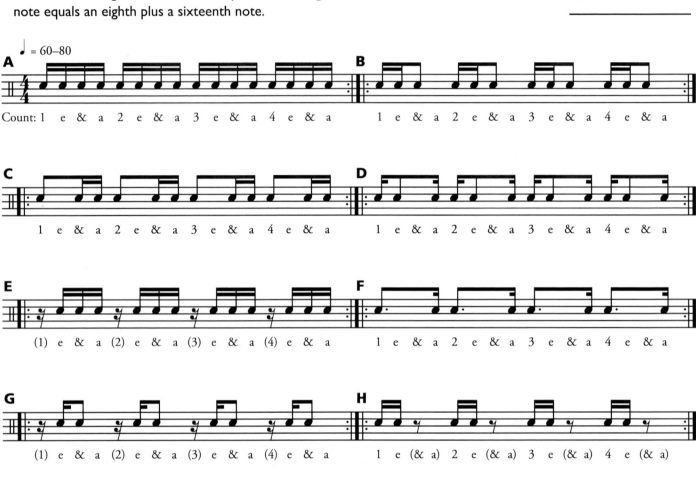

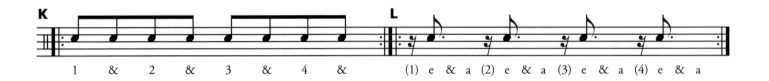

Two-Handed Sixteenth-Note Rock Beats

Two-handed sixteenth-note beats are used when the tempo of a song is too fast for one hand to play all the sixteenth notes.

Use a single-stroke roll between the hi-hat and the snare drum for all of these exercises. Once they become comfortable, work on speeding up the tempo.

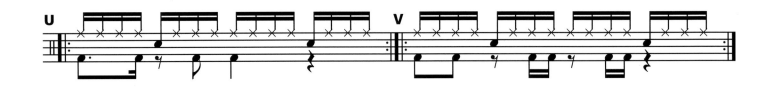

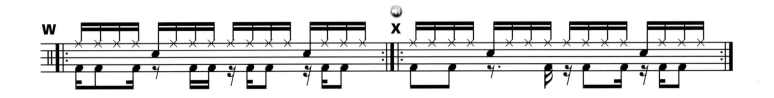

Sixteenth-Note Grouping Fills

Below are some fills using the different sixteenth-note groupings that you learned earlier. It helps to count all the sixteenth notes in these fills until you are comfortable with them.

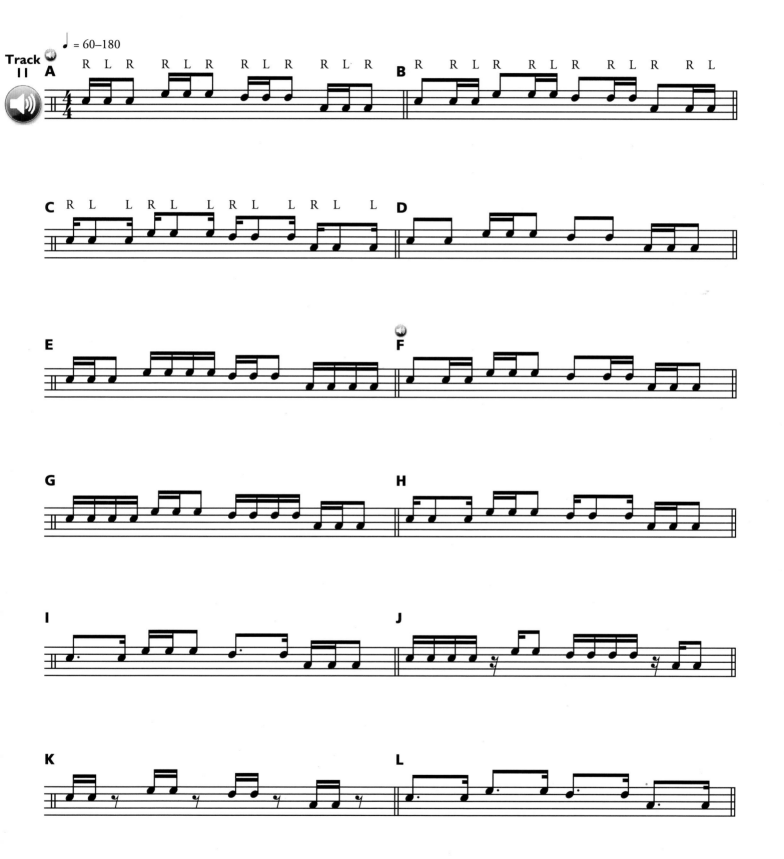

M

N R L   R L   R L   R L

O

P

Q

R

S

T

U

V

W

X

Sixteenth-Note Tom Tom Beats

Following are some great sixteenth-note tom tom beats.
Keep a close eye on the stickings and have fun.

Chapter 5: Changing the Feel

Half-Time Feel

The term *half-time feel* refers to a more relaxed sounding beat. In a normal beat, you hear the snare drum on beats 2 and 4 (this is known as the *backbeat*). In a half-time feel, you hear the snare drum on beat 3, or in some cases, just on beat 4.

It is important to remember that the tempo does not change, just the feel. So, do not confuse the term "half-time feel" with "half-time." Half-time means actually cutting the tempo in half, while half-time feel maintains the same tempo and just changes the feel.

After learning half-time feels, try practicing a standard rock beat with the snare on beats 2 and 4, and then switch directly to a half-time feel.

PHOTO BY JEFFREY MAYER/COURTESY OF STAR FILE PHOTO, INC.

Ginger Baker (b. 1939) was the drummer for the 1960s British rock group Cream, which also included bassist Jack Bruce and guitarist Eric Clapton. Cream defined the power-trio approach to rock music and pushed the envelope in rock improvisation. In addition to fiery, show-stealing drum solos, Baker's innovative style incorporated odd time signatures and many different "feels" that were integral to Cream's unique and progressive sound.

The following consists of eighth-note half-time rock feels
with the snare drum on beat 3.

Now, let's look at some half-time feels with the snare on beat 4.

Double-Time Feel

A *double-time feel* is when we play the snare drum on all four beats (1–2–3–4) or on all the *offbeats* (the "ands," or &s). This produces a very powerful and energetic driving beat. Even though these beats tend to sound like a "caveman" style of drumming when we first learn them, with practice, they will start to groove and sound musical. Some songs may require a double-time feel for their entirety, while others have a short double-time section to build the intensity. Remember, the tempo does not change when you go to a double-time feel. Do not confuse double-time *feel* with true *double time* (where the tempo is actually doubled). It just *feels* like the tempo was doubled. Always practice with a click track to fully understand how to utilize these grooves.

Good examples of beats with a double-time feel include "Pretty Woman" by Roy Orbison, "Satisfaction" by the Rolling Stones, and many classic Motown tracks.

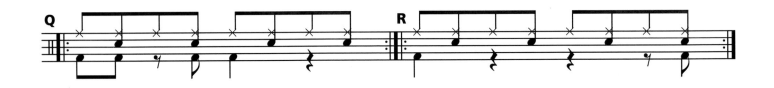

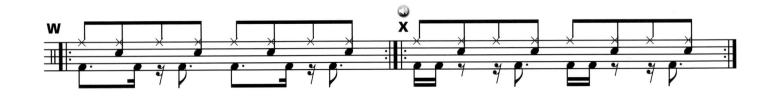

Chapter 6: Funk Rock

Funk music is a highly rhythmic style that evolved from soul and R&B. Funk drummers began playing more *syncopated,* or off-beat, snare and bass drum patterns, usually against a straighter cymbal rhythm.

A great example of early funk is the music of "The Godfather of Soul," James Brown. Brown's early drummers included Clyde Stubblefield and John "Jabo" Starks. Check out their playing to hear how they laid down these great grooves in the funk style.

Bands such as Tower of Power, with David Garibaldi on drums, were really stretching the rhythmic muscle with funk music. The drum parts consisted of "broken" cymbal patterns, using rudiments such as the paradiddle and its various permutations. *Ghost notes* were often played on the snare drum to really enhance the groove. You'll also hear many *linear patterns* (see page 56) throughout many eras of funk.

Today, the funk influence is strong in the music of funk rock bands like the Red Hot Chili Peppers.

Some other great funk bands to check out are: Sly & the Family Stone, the Meters, Parliament/Funkadelic, Earth, Wind & Fire, the Commodores, and Average White Band.

The exercises in this chapter will help you fully understand this great and fun style of music.

The Red Hot Chili Peppers began playing their unique mixture of funk, rap, and punk in the late 1970s and early 1980s. While they maintained a cult following for years, their first real commercial success came with the release of Mother's Milk *in 1989. Since then, their popularity has continued to grow, and they serve as a great example of what happens when funk meets rock.*

Funk Rock Grooves

Following are some basic funk grooves. They feature *syncopation*, or offbeats on the snare drum and/or bass drum. You'll notice that these beats are more complex and varied than previous beats you've practiced. The snare drum will be played on beats other than 2 and 4, and the bass drum will have sixteenth-note syncopations as well.

Drummers like Chad Smith of the Red Hot Chili Peppers and Travis Barker of Blink 182 use these types of grooves in their playing. Check out recordings of Clyde Stubblefield and Jabo Starks, who both played with James Brown, for good examples of these grooves.

Grooves with Ghost Notes

Ghost notes, when played properly, can add spice to your grooves. The notes that you see in parentheses (♩) should be played on the snare drum as softly as possible. When playing a ghost note, keep your stick as low as possible to the drum head.

The snare drum is *accented* or played louder on beats 2 and 4. Practice these beats slowly at first, focusing on the dynamic range of your snare notes. Have fun!

(♩) = Ghost note

Paradiddles on the Drumset—Grooves and Fills

In this section, we'll employ the paradiddle (RLRR, LRLL) around the drumset to create some very funky grooves and amazing fills. All of these exercises are written with sixteenth notes. Many drummers never venture into creating grooves and fills with the paradiddle, but once you get a grasp of these patterns, you'll be glad you did. The paradiddle creates a funky pattern between the cymbal and the snare drum, and you'll notice in the examples below that the accents played with the left hand on beats 2 and 4 produce a cool backbeat effect.

All of these patterns maintain the paradiddle throughout, except that the bass drum pattern will change for each exercise. When playing the fills, keep the paradiddle consistent and make sure you are playing the proper drum or cymbal.

Drummers such as Mike Portnoy of Dream Theater, Neil Peart of Rush, and David Garibaldi of Tower of Power use these types of grooves and fills in their playing.

Grooves

Use the paradiddle sticking for all of the following fills.

Fills

"○" indicates open hi-hat

Permutated Paradiddle Funk Grooves

Permutated paradiddle grooves are advanced funk studies. To permutate means to mix things up or create a new combination of the original pattern. If you look closely at the first exercise below, you'll see that the normal paradiddle begins on the "a" of beat 1. We are simply starting the paradiddle on a different note. These grooves are great for creating crazy rock beats. Drummers like Mike Portnoy and Virgil Donati of Steve Vai use variations of these beats.

Funky Two-Handed Sixteenth-Note Grooves

Funky two-handed sixteenth-note grooves are great when you want to play funk at fast tempos. Playing sixteenth notes on the hi-hat gives a real driving effect to these grooves. One of the best tracks using this style is "Ain't Nobody" by Chaka Kahn with John "J. R." Robinson on drums.

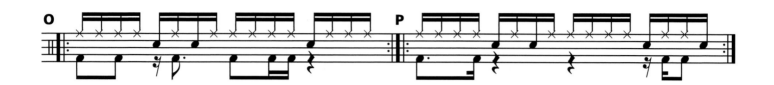

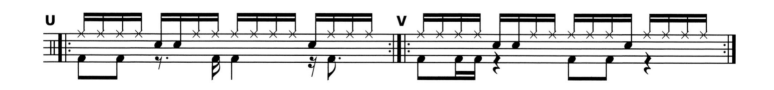

Funky Cymbal Grooves

In this section, we will take a look at how we can change some basic grooves by adding new rhythms to the hi-hat or ride cymbal. The bass drum remains fairly simple so you can focus on the new cymbal patterns. These may be challenging at first, so practice them slowly, and work on speeding them up.

Two Surface-Riding Funk Rock Grooves

These exercises consist of *riding* (playing) on two different *surfaces* (cymbals)—the hi-hat and the ride cymbal. You will use the single-stroke roll for all of these exercises, and keep a close watch on which hand plays the ride and which plays the hi-hat.

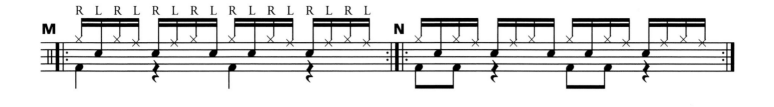

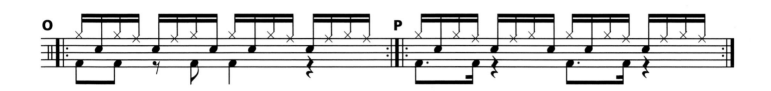

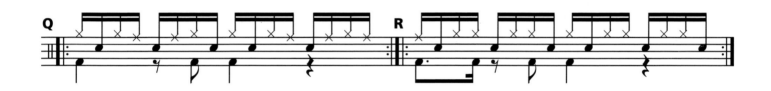

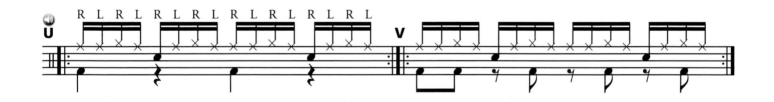

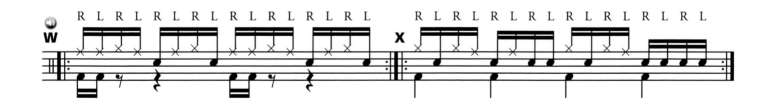

Linear Funk Rock Grooves

Linear grooves are created when you play every limb (arms and legs) independently. You'll never strike two sounds at once in a linear groove. This exercise will help you develop complete separation when playing grooves. These may seem a bit strange at first, but be patient and keep each note separate from one another. Drummers who use linear beats in their playing include Neil Peart, Bill Bruford of Yes and King Crimson, and Mike Portnoy.

Chapter 7: Eighth-Note Triplets

Eighth-note triplets, also known simply as *triplets*, are a rhythmic value that is counted as follows: "1–trip–let, 2–trip–let, 3–trip–let, 4–trip–let." They are written as groups of three eighth notes with the numeral 3 above or below each grouping. Triplets divide the quarter note into three equal parts.

Count: 1 trip - let 2 trip - let 3 trip - let 4 trip - let

In the example to the right, we play only "1–trip–let, 3–trip–let." Rest for the entirety of beats 2 and 4 (2–trip–let and 4–trip–let).

Count: 1 trip - let (2 trip - let) 3 trip - let (4 trip - let)

In this example, we play "1–trip–let, 2–trip–let" and rest on beats 3 and 4.

Count: 1 trip - let 2 trip - let (3 trip - let) (4 trip - let)

In this example, we play the first and last notes of each triplet.

Count: 1 (trip) - let 2 (trip) - let 3 (trip) - let 4 (trip) - let

Finally, let's rest on the onbeats and play only the "trip–let" of each beat.

Count: (1) trip - let (2) trip - let (3) trip - let (4) trip - let

$\frac{12}{8}$ Time

The $\frac{12}{8}$ time signature creates a pulse similar to triplets. Notice the 3s do not appear above the groups of notes when we are counting $\frac{12}{8}$. You will find that some authors prefer $\frac{12}{8}$ while others prefer $\frac{4}{4}$ using eighth-note triplets. In this book, we will use $\frac{4}{4}$ for consistency. Also, $\frac{12}{8}$ time is usually used for slower tempos.

Count: 1 2 3 4 5 6 7 8 9 10 11 12

Eighth-Note Triplet Exercises

Here are a series of exercises to help you develop eighth-note triplet rhythms. Some of these will combine triplets and quarter notes, while others combine triplets and various rests. Count all the triplets aloud while practicing. You will see these patterns used in beats, fills, and solos in the upcoming chapters.

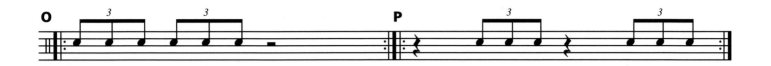

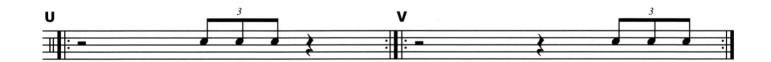

Eighth-Note Triplet Rock Beats

Triplet rock beats are commonly used in blues rock, 1950s rock, classic rock, and many current styles of rock. Lots of songs by Elvis Presley, Stevie Ray Vaughan, Ray Charles, and others use triplet beats. One very popular song using this rhythm is "Hold the Line" by Toto, featuring Jeff Porcaro on drums.

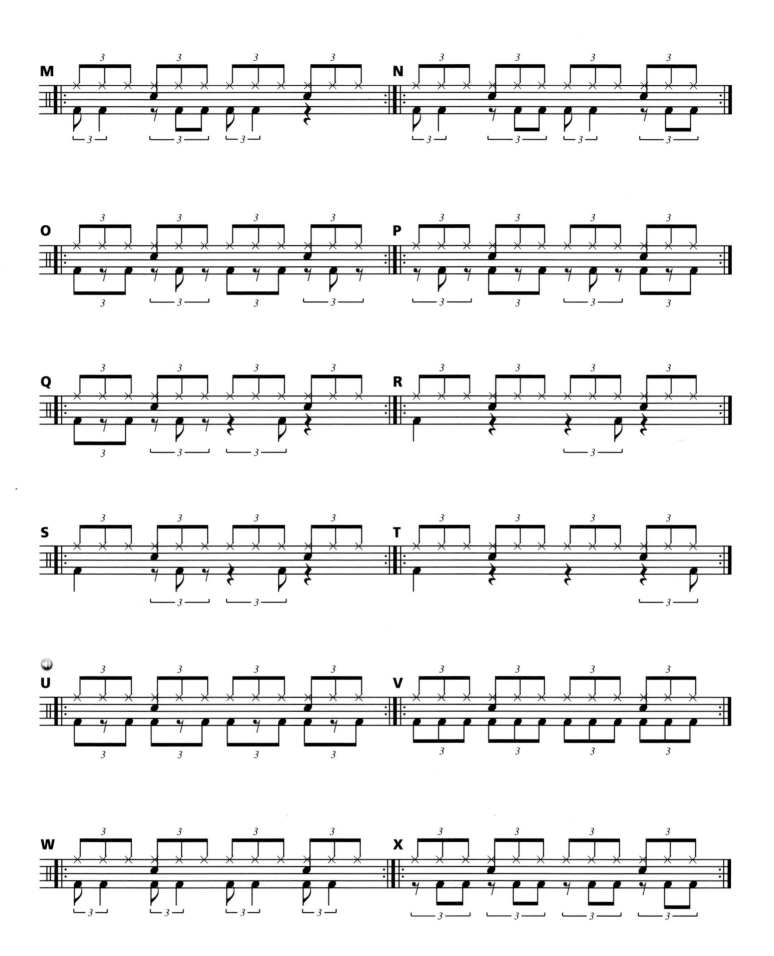

The Shuffle

The *shuffle* is a great groove that is based on eighth-note triplets. You play all of the triplets except for the middle triplet ("trip") of each group.

Many famous songs such as "Roadhouse Blues," "Blue Suede Shoes," "Some Kind of Wonderful," and many songs by Stevie Ray Vaughan use the shuffle rhythm. Count all the triplets when practicing these.

In these examples, you will add more snare notes to the shuffle pattern.

♩ = 100–150

Track 27

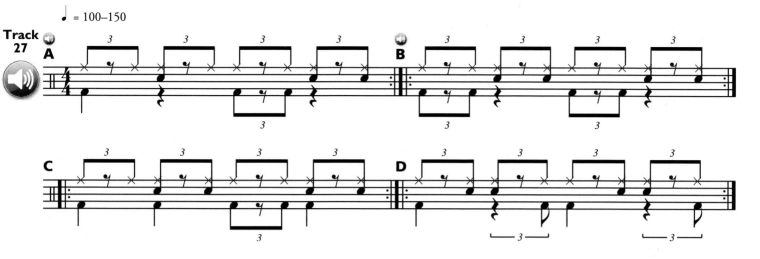

These are examples of *double shuffle*—both hands play the shuffle.

Track 28

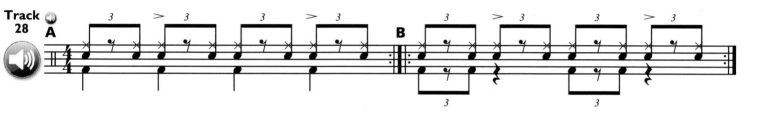

Here, we add some ghost notes to start creating funky shuffle beats.

Track 29

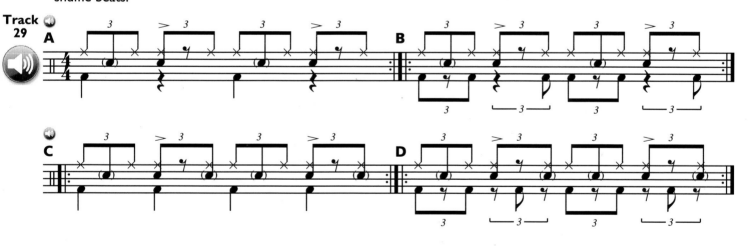

Below are examples of the *backwards shuffle*—a strange little beat, but common in blues. The snare drum hits on the "let" of each triplet.

Track 30

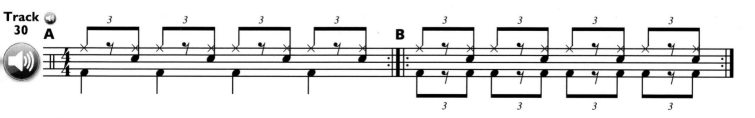

Half-Time Feel Shuffle

The *half-time feel shuffle* is a great rock beat. You play the shuffle pattern on the cymbal, but the main snare backbeat is on beat 3. This beat has driven many great rock songs such as "Fool in the Rain" by Led Zeppelin and "Rosanna" by Toto.

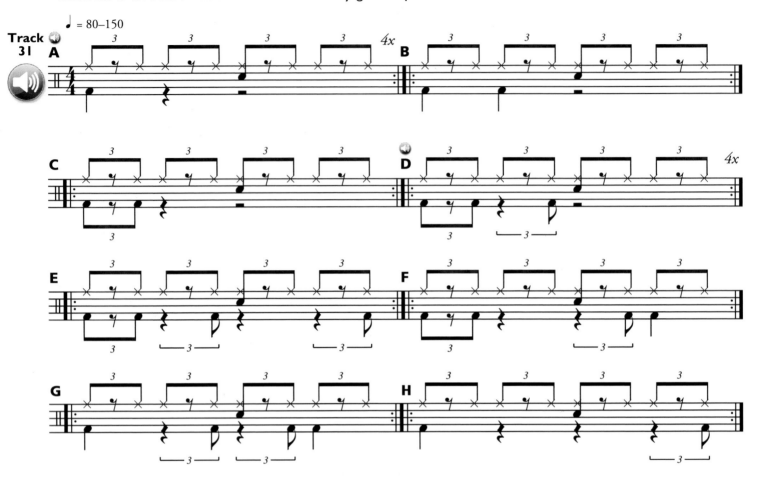

The *Bernard Purdie half-time feel shuffle* is distinguished by the ghost notes on the snare. This beat can be heard on "Babylon Sisters" and "Home at Last" by Steely Dan. Be sure to accent beat 3 and play the ghost notes as softly as you can.

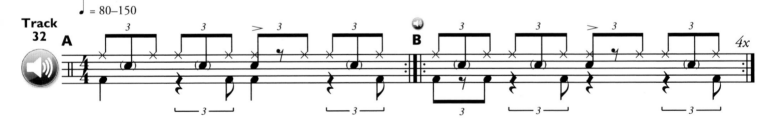

The *Jeff Porcaro half-time feel shuffle* is the two-bar pattern played on "Rosanna" by Toto. It's similar to the Bernard Purdie shuffle, but with four ghost notes per bar and a more syncopated bass drum pattern. The beat is tricky at first, so be patient.

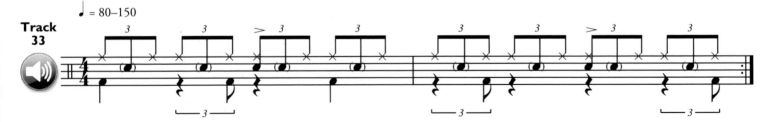

Triplet Fills

Triplet fills can be used with eighth-note triplet beats such as the shuffle and half-time feel shuffle, and even with the eighth-note and sixteenth-note beats you've learned. These fills are very versatile and can be heard in all styles of music. Try to get creative with the sticking patterns for these fills. You'll notice that some fills have sticking patterns other than the single-stroke roll. The reason for this is so they can be played faster around the drumset.

M

N

O

P

Q

R

S

T

U

V

W

X

Triplet Tom Tom Beats

Following are some triplet tom tom beats. A drummer who uses these beats quite often is Green Day's drummer, Tré Cool. Listen to the songs "Holiday" and "Hitchin' a Ride." Watch your stickings with these beats and remember to count the triplets.

Chapter 8: Sixteenth-Note Triplets

Sixteenth-note triplets consist of six notes to the quarter note. You will also be counting the regular eighth note in sixteenth-note triplets. Look at the examples below to see how sixteenth-note triplets fit together with the quarter note and the eighth note.

Sixteenth-Note Triplets

A

Count: 1 trip-let & trip-let 2 trip-let & trip-let 3 trip-let & trip-let 4 trip-let & trip-let

B

Count: 1 trip-let & trip-let 2 trip-let & trip-let 3 trip-let & trip-let 4 trip-let & trip-let

C

Count: 1 trip-let & trip-let 2 trip-let & trip-let 3 trip-let & trip-let 4 trip-let & trip-let

D

Count: 1 trip-let & trip-let 2 trip-let & trip-let 3 trip-let & trip-let 4 trip-let & trip-let

E

Count: 1 trip-let & trip-let 2 trip-let & trip-let 3 trip-let & trip-let 4 trip-let & trip-let

Sixteenth-Note Triplet Exercises

Practice these exercises on a pad or a snare drum. Be sure to count the sixteenth-note triplet rhythm aloud. You'll notice various rests as well as quarter notes, eighth notes, and sixteenth notes.

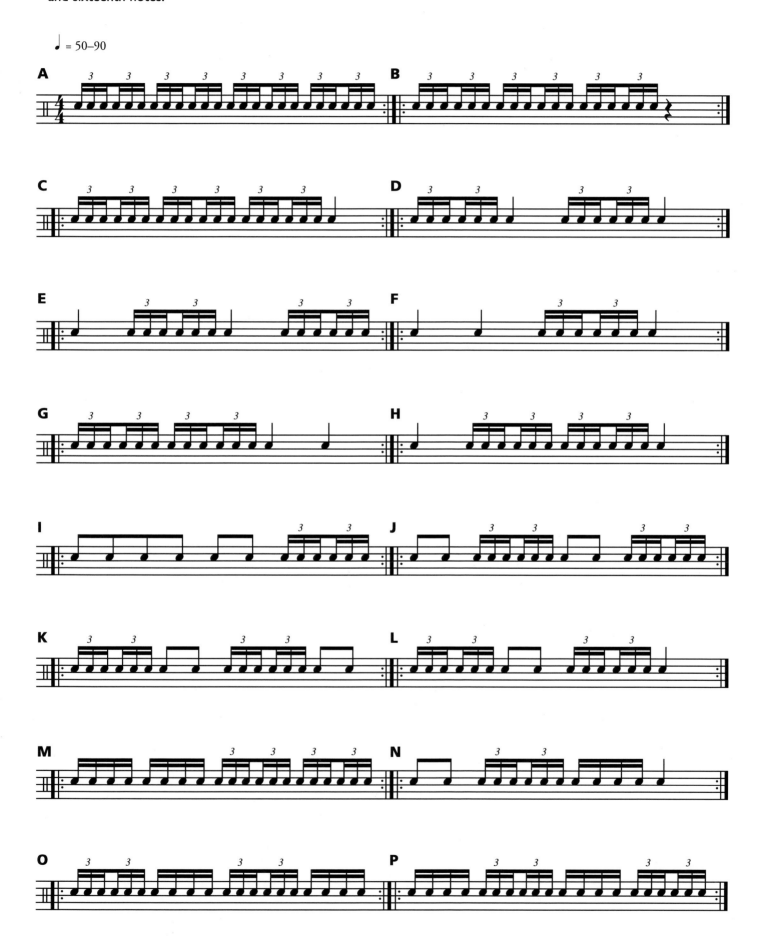

Sixteenth-Note Triplet Rock Beats

Below are examples of beats played by great progressive rock drummers such as Mike Portnoy, Neil Peart, and Danny Carey of Tool.

Sixteenth-Note Triplet Fills

Here are some sixteenth-note triplet fills around the drumset. You can use these fills with any of the beats you've already learned, and they can be used in any style of music, including rock, heavy metal, funk, pop, country, Latin, and jazz.

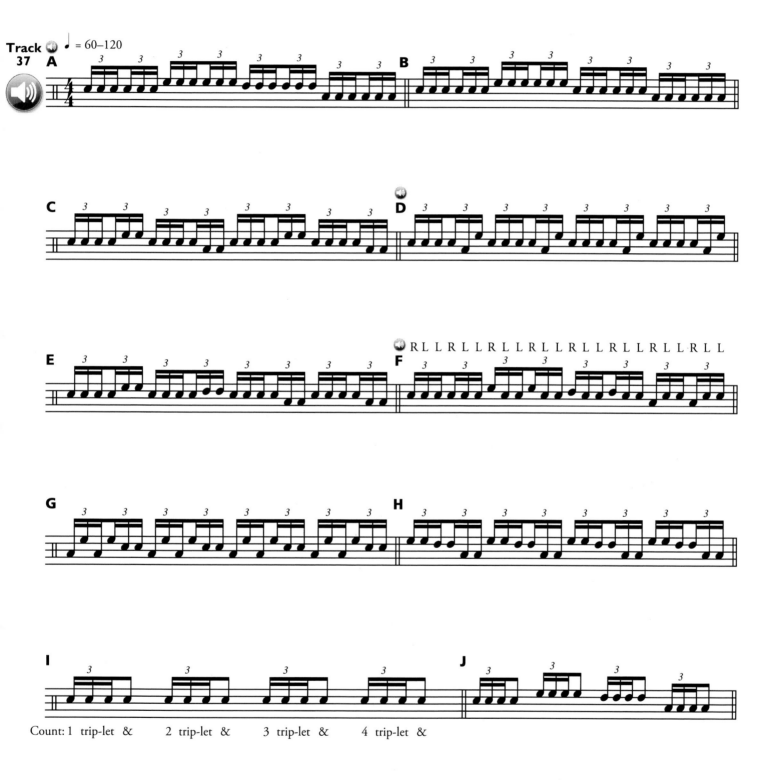

Count: 1   & trip-let   2   & trip-let   3   & trip-let   4   & trip-let

Tom Tom Beats with Sixteenth-Note Triplets

Check out the following examples of powerful and driving tom tom beats with sixteenth-note triplets. Many progressive rock drummers use these beats.

Chapter 9: Thirty-Second Notes and Rests

Thirty-second notes divide a bar of $\frac{4}{4}$ into 32 equal parts. Each quarter note is divided into eight thirty-second notes. They can be counted "1–e–&–a–&–e–&–a, 2–e–&–a–&–e–&–a, 3–e–&–a–&–e–&–a, 4 e & a & e & a." This is the easiest way to count all 32 notes. Be patient and start slowly. The first example shows how thirty-second notes line up with the quarter-note rhythm.

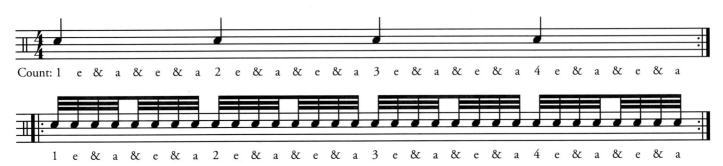

Count: 1 e & a & e & a 2 e & a & e & a 3 e & a & e & a 4 e & a & e & a

1 e & a & e & a 2 e & a & e & a 3 e & a & e & a 4 e & a & e & a

Below is a pattern of eight thirty-second notes followed by eight *thirty-second rests* (♼). Writing the rests in this way is not considered proper music notation (see below).

The proper way to write the above exercise is to use a quarter rest, which is equal in duration to eight thirty-second rests.

Thirty-second rests are used to indicate a silence in a group of thirty-second notes, as in the following example.

Count:1 e & a & e & a 2 e & a & e & a 3 e & a & e & a 4 e & a & e & a

As a rule of thumb, music should be notated using the largest value rest possible, so long as the larger "pulse" of the music can be clearly followed.

Count: 1 e & a (& e & a) 2 e & a (& e & a) 3 e & a (& e & a) 4 e & a (& e & a)

Here's another thirty-second note grouping.

1 (e & a) & e & a 2 (e & a) & e & a 3 (e & a) & e & a 4 (e & a) & e & a

Thirty-Second Note Exercise

Practice the following exercises one bar at a time on a practice pad or snare drum. Be sure to count all the thirty-second notes, even if you are not playing all of them, as in some of the examples below. As an added challenge, try playing them all nonstop once you are comfortable with these new rhythms.

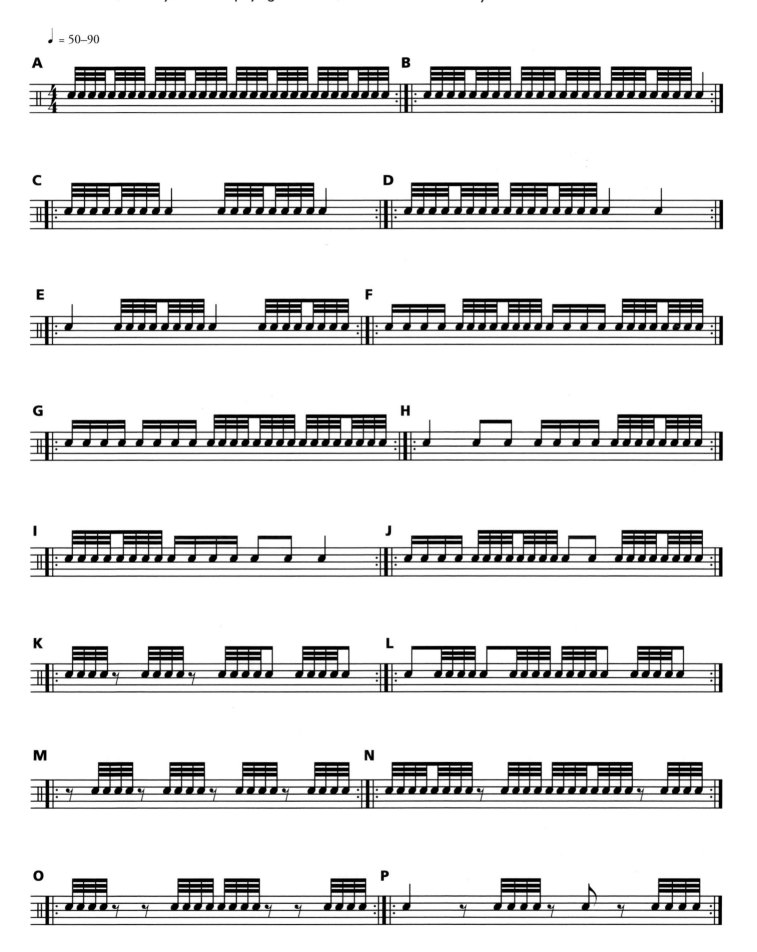

Thirty-Second Note Beats

Following are some advanced thirty-second note beats. You will be using the single-stroke roll and the double- stroke roll for these fills. Get comfortable with the hand patterns first before adding the bass drum. Have fun!

Thirty-Second Note Fills

Thirty-second note fills are a great addition to the drummer's toolbox. Once you develop your hand speed, these exercises will work great with any beat you've already learned. You can also practice these in continuous fashion and in different combinations to start creating great drum solo ideas.

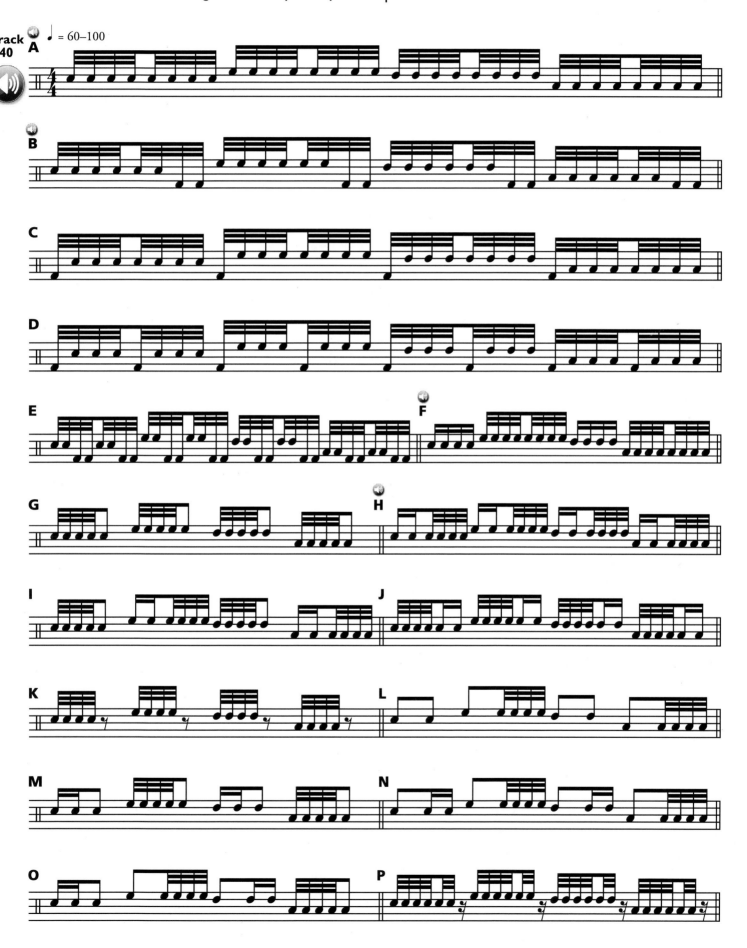

Track 40

♩ = 60–100

Subdividing the Beat

Now that you've learned and practiced all of the note values—from quarter notes to thirty-second notes—it's time to put them all together. The following exercises show how to divide the beat with different note values. In the notation, the quarter-note pulse is represented by the bass drum, but on the recording the beat is kept with the metronome. Practice these with a metronome slowly at first.

Track 41 A ♩ = 60–90

This exercise is similar to the one above, but in the reverse order.

B ♩ = 60–90

Practice this six-bar exercise slowly at first, and eventually start speeding it up.

Track 42

♩ = 60–90

The following exercises should be practiced one bar at a time. The note value changes every beat. These can be quite challenging, so start slowly with the metronome and count aloud. You can get adventurous and move these exercises around the drumset to create some crazy fills.

♩ = 60–90

Track 43

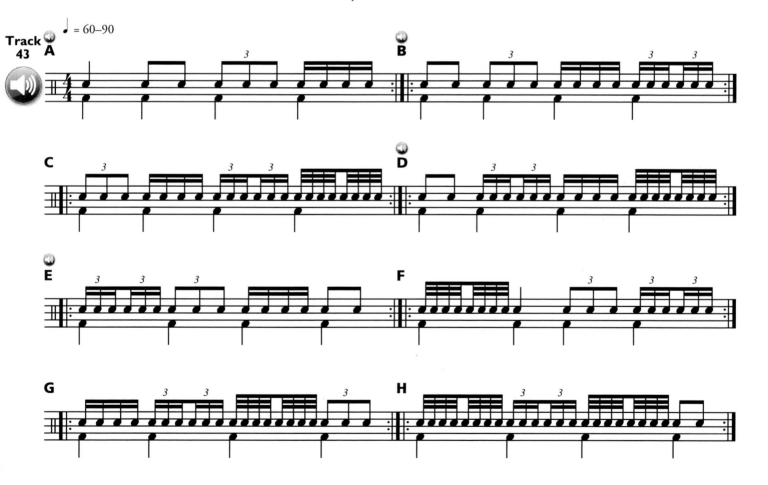

Chapter 10: Bass Drum Applications

Bass Drum Development

This exercise will help you develop a more accurate and precise placement of the bass drum using sixteenth notes, while maintaining a straight eighth-note rock beat. Start slowly and gradually develop your speed over time.

Track 44

♩ = 60–85

Bass Drum Workout

These are great, usable drum beats that can be heard in many styles of rock. The purpose of this exercise is to get you playing cool grooves at fast tempos. Start slowly and gradually increase your speed.

♩ = 80–130

Double-Bass Grooves

If you have a *double-bass pedal* (or two bass drums), you can play rapid bass-drum patterns using both feet. For all of the following grooves, play eighth notes on the ride cymbal (or closed hi-hat) and the snare on beats 2 and 4. The grooves recorded in the audio are repeated four times. Drummers who made double-bass popular are Mike Portnoy, Lars Ulrich, Vinnie Paul of Pantera, Joey Jordison of Slipknot, Chris Adler of Lamb of God, Terry Bozzio of Frank Zappa, and many more.

Double-Bass Notation

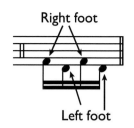

The following examples, with the exception of the last two, all feature triplet rhythms in the double bass. In the recording, the examples are repeated four times.

Double-Bass Fills

Double-bass fills can be used with any of the beats you've already learned. Be certain that your hands and feet all play with the same intensity and clarity. Practice these fills one bar at a time on their own, then try incorporating them into your favorite rock beat.

Chapter 11: Hi-Hat Applications

Opening the Hi-Hat

Opening and closing the hi-hat while playing grooves is a great way to add color and spice to your playing. Not only does the hi-hat make a nice sound when it's opened properly, but it also infuses the groove with a new rhythmic flow.

Here's how to get started.

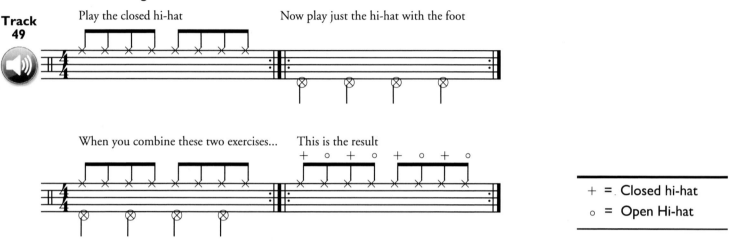

+ =	Closed hi-hat
o =	Open Hi-hat

Here are some great beats featuring this technique.

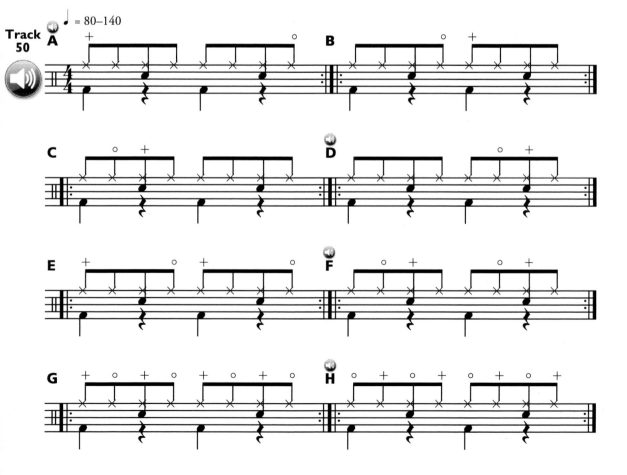

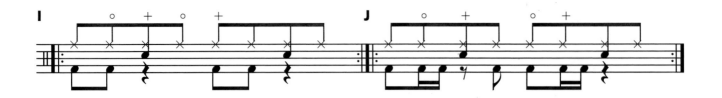

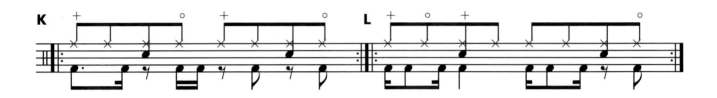

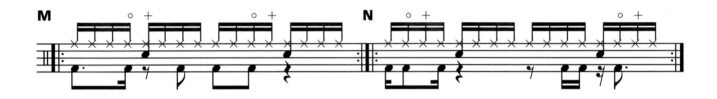

R L R L R L R L R L R L R L R L R L

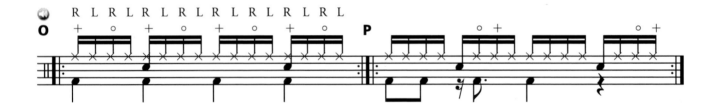

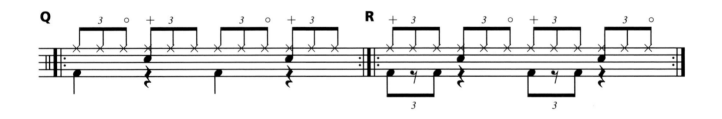

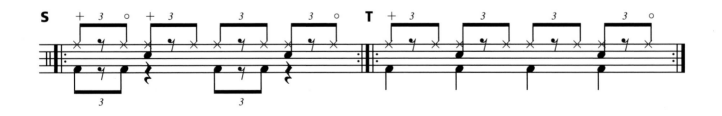

Adding the Hi-Hat Foot to Beats 2 and 4

It's time to incorporate the hi-hat foot into some popular beats. By adding the hi-hat to beats 2 and 4, you are emphasizing the backbeat and creating a new sound on your drumset. Play the ride cymbal with your right hand and simply press down on the hi-hat pedal whenever you hit the snare drum.

Adding Hi-Hat Foot Quarter Notes

Adding hi-hat foot quarter notes to popular rock beats can be a challenge. By doing so, you will help lock in the time of your groove and keep the performance sounding tight. This technique will also add a new sound to your playing. Once you've practiced these, try going back to beats you've previously learned and add hi-hat foot quarter notes to those as well.

Adding Hi-Hat Foot Eighth Notes

Here's a great hi-hat foot workout. You simply play your hi-hat foot along with your ride cymbal notes. By doing this, you will add excitement and that extra push your groove may need. Drummers have been using this technique for decades. Check out John Bonham, Terry Bozzio, Keith Moon of the Who, Vinnie Colaiuta of Allan Holdsworth, and many more.

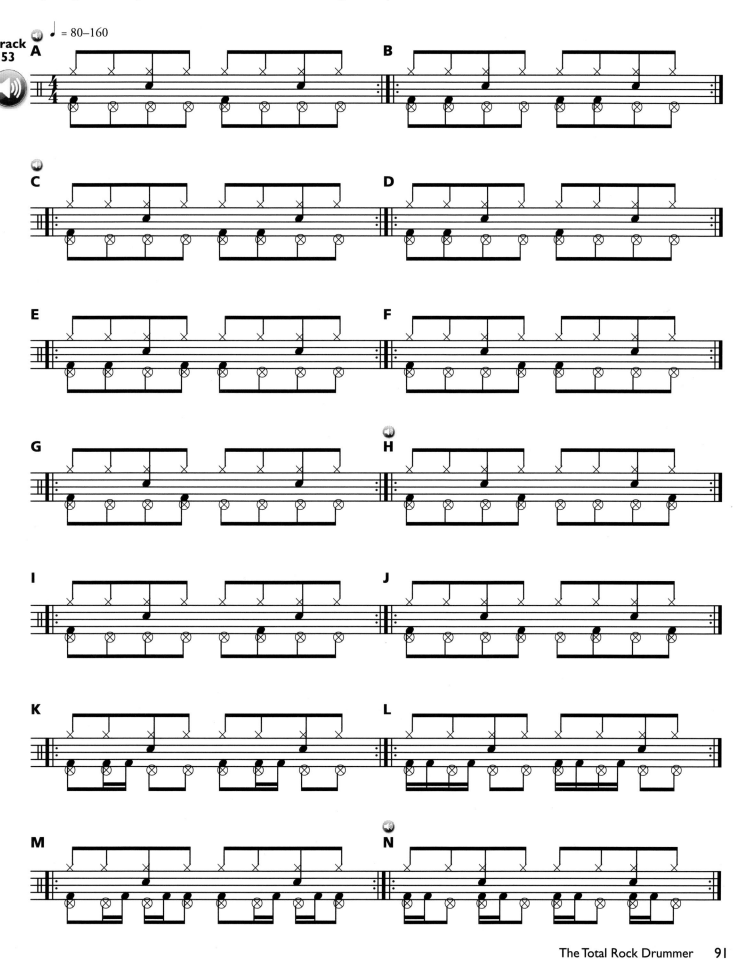

Adding the Hi-Hat Foot to the "Ands"

Adding the hi-hat foot to the "ands," or offbeats, is a serious challenge for many drummers. The way modern drumming is evolving, more and more drummers are using this technique in their playing. Drummers such as Thomas Lang, Virgil Donati, and Marco Minnemann, use this hi-hat technique to add an "off-beat" feel to otherwise simple beats.

Hi-Hat Barks

The difference between opening the hi-hat and a *hi-hat bark* is that a bark is a shorter, snappier hit on the hi-hat, played in time to create a *staccato* (short, detached) opening. The recorded examples will help you understand the sound of the bark. The following exercises will have

you barking on the hi-hat with two-handed sixteenth-note grooves. Drummers who play great hi-hat barks are Jeff Porcaro, John "J. R." Robinson, Mike Portnoy, Neil Peart, and David Garibaldi.

Chapter 12: Six-Beat Meter

Rock Beats in 6/8

We begin this chapter with rock beats in 6/8. This simply means there are six eighth notes to the bar. Each time you see an eighth note, it receives one count. Be sure to count 1–2–3–4–5–6 in each measure (or you can count 1–2–3, 2–2–3, emphasizing a two-beat pulse in each measure). In the recording, the beats are repeated four times.

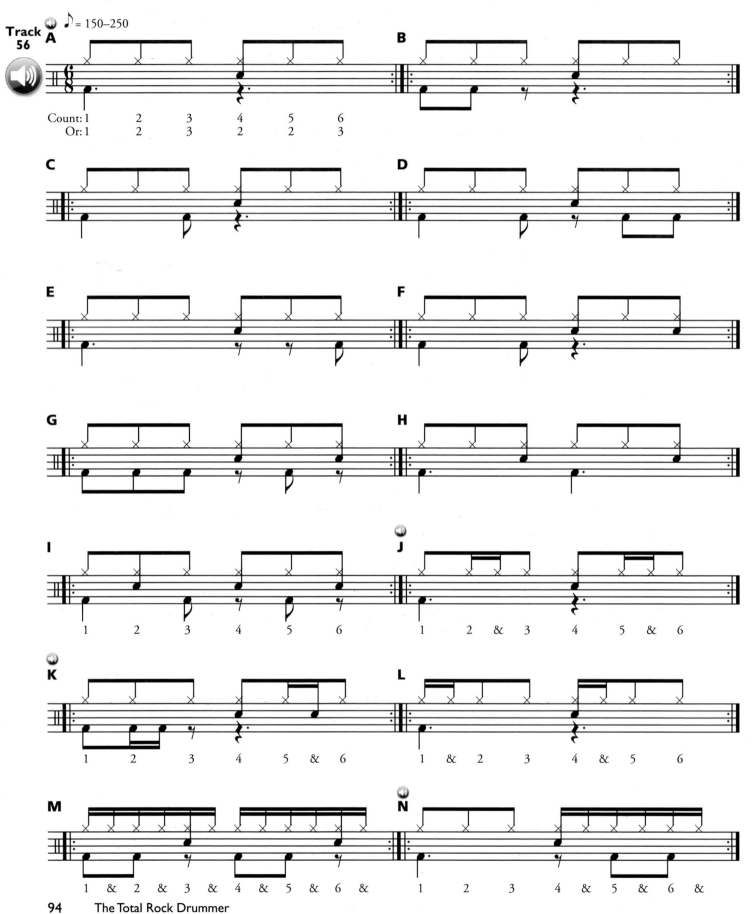

Fills in ⁶⁄₈

Now that you've learned ⁶⁄₈ beats, it's time to start practicing some ⁶⁄₈ fills around the drums. Practice these one bar at a time, and then go back and incorporate them into the ⁶⁄₈ beats.

Track 57 ♪ = 180–250

The Total Rock Drummer   95

Grooves in $\frac{6}{4}$

The following grooves are played in $\frac{6}{4}$. They are two beats longer than a regular $\frac{4}{4}$ beat. You can count all six quarter notes, or you can divide the bar into smaller sections. An example would be 1–2–3–4, 1–2 or 1–2–3, 1–2–3, etc. It usually depends on how the song is written. For the following exercises, count all six quarter notes to become comfortable with them. Tunes like "Fell on Black Days" by Soundgarden, and "Fear of a Blank Planet" by Porcupine Tree are great examples of $\frac{6}{4}$ grooves.

Track 58

$\quad \bullet = 90–150$

Count: 1 & 2 & 3 & 4 & 5 & 6 &

K   R L R L R L R L etc.

Fills in $\frac{6}{4}$

Fills in $\frac{6}{4}$ can be used with the $\frac{6}{4}$ beats you've learned. These may seem long at first, because they are two beats longer than any of the $\frac{4}{4}$ fills you've practiced. The key is to count so you know where the quarter note is as you practice these fills. These examples incorporate many different rhythms to keep the fills interesting and challenging.

Track 59 ♩ = 90–150

Chapter 13: Odd Time Signatures

Grooves in 7/8

Odd time signatures do not divide the measure into "typical" patterns such as two, three, or four beats. 7/8 grooves are the most popular odd-time beats. One way to think of 7/8 is to realize that 4/4 is equivalent 8/8. With this in mind, if you drop one eighth note from 8/8, you get 7/8. Therefore, you can think of 7/8 as 4/4 minus an eighth note. Drummers such as

Neil Peart, Danny Carey, Mike Portnoy, Billy Cobham, Phil Collins, Terry Bozzio, and Vinnie Colaiuta are known for making 7/8 sound great. There are many ways to count 7/8, and other odd-time signatures, so for most cases in this book, beaming of the notes is avoided. For the sake of simplicity, we will count the following exercises 1–2–3–4–5–6–7.

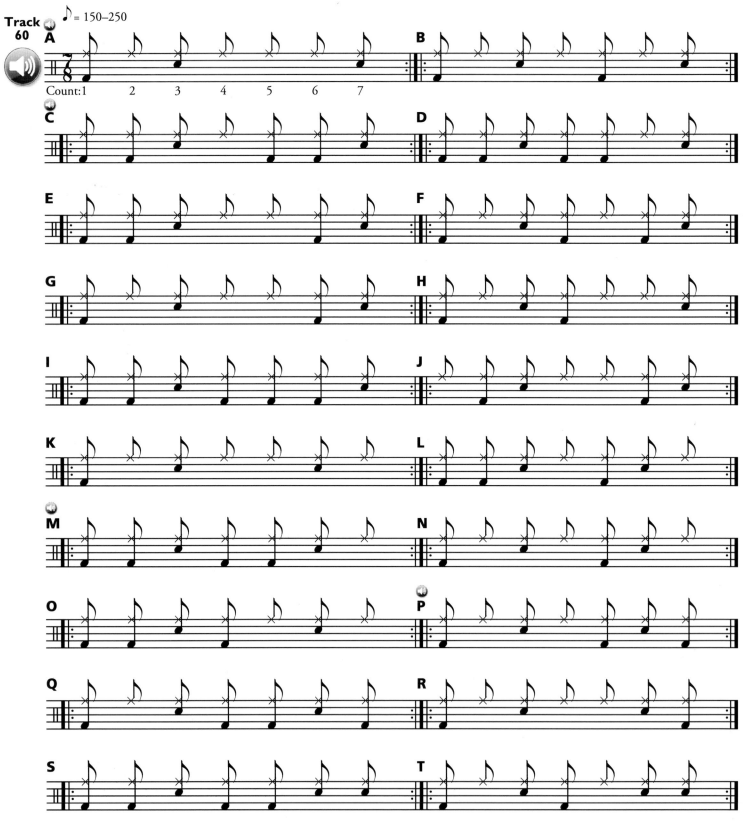

Fills in $\frac{7}{8}$

Here are some great examples of fills in $\frac{7}{8}$ time. Practice these one bar at a time, then try to incorporate them into $\frac{7}{8}$ grooves.

Grooves in $\frac{7}{4}$

In $\frac{7}{4}$ time, you count seven quarter notes to the measure. Grooves in $\frac{7}{4}$ are rather long, because they are three beats longer than a $\frac{4}{4}$ groove. Counting to seven will help you get the flow of these grooves. Below are examples with quarter notes, eighth notes, sixteenth notes, and triplets on the cymbal. The song "Money" by Pink Floyd is a great example of a groove in $\frac{7}{4}$.

Track 62

Fills in $\frac{7}{4}$

The following fills in $\frac{7}{4}$ should be practiced one measure at a time. Once you are comfortable, begin incorporating them into $\frac{7}{4}$ grooves. These fills include flams, quarter notes, eighth notes, sixteenth notes, triplets, and sixteenth-note triplets to keep things interesting. Have fun!

Grooves in 5/4

Grooves in 5/4 time can be counted simply by adding one quarter note to 4/4 time. Each quarter note receives one count. The snare drum can vary in 5/4 grooves, as you'll see in the examples below. You'll also find a 5/4 triplet beat and a 5/4 shuffle below.

The most popular song written in 5/4 time is the original version of the "Mission Impossible" theme.

Track 64

102   The Total Rock Drummer

Fills in $\frac{5}{4}$

It's time to start practicing some fills in $\frac{5}{4}$ time. Remember that they are one quarter note longer than $\frac{4}{4}$ fills. Practice them one measure at a time, and then incorporate them into grooves in $\frac{5}{4}$.

Track 65   ♩ = 90–180

Grooves in $\frac{5}{8}$

$\frac{5}{8}$ is the shortest time signature in this chapter, one eighth note shorter than $\frac{6}{8}$. Count "1–2–3–4–5," with each eighth note receiving one beat. Placing the snare drum on beat 3 is very common in $\frac{5}{8}$. The following exercises have varied snare and bass drum patterns so you can become comfortable playing any $\frac{5}{8}$ beat.

Track 66   ♪ = 100–200

Fills in 5/8

These 5/8 fills should be practiced one measure at a time, and then you can incorporate them into 5/8 grooves. Remember, in 5/8 time, the eighth note receives the beat.

Grooves in $\frac{9}{8}$

$\frac{9}{8}$ grooves are basically $\frac{4}{4}$ (or $\frac{8}{8}$) plus one eighth note. You'll notice that many of these beats have a triplet feel to them, almost like triplets in $\frac{3}{4}$ time. The idea is to make sure you are playing all nine eighth notes. You can either count to nine for each exercise, or divide these beats into three sections of three: "1–2–3, 1–2–3, 1–2–3." Try both methods of counting and decide which one is easier for you.

106   The Total Rock Drummer

Fills in $\frac{9}{8}$

These $\frac{9}{8}$ fills should be practiced one measure at a time, and then incorporated into the $\frac{9}{8}$ grooves you learned on the previous page. As with the $\frac{9}{8}$ grooves, you can either count all nine eighth notes in a measure or divide the bar into three groups of three.

Grooves in $\frac{11}{8}$

Learning grooves with large time signatures such as $\frac{11}{8}$ can be challenging at first because counting all 11 eighth notes may be confusing. Many drummers subdivide the beat into smaller sections of twos, threes, fours, fives, sixes, and sevens. Depending on how the song is phrased, the $\frac{11}{8}$ beat can be counted in several different ways. Below are several examples of playing $\frac{11}{8}$ grooves with different counting methods. Notice that each grouping will always total 11 eighth notes. For an example of $\frac{11}{8}$, listen to "Heavy Resin" by Karizma, featuring Vinnie Colaiuta on drums.

Track 70 ♪ = 130–230

Fills in $\frac{11}{8}$

$\frac{11}{8}$ fills can be incorporated into grooves in $\frac{11}{8}$. Use a metronome to ensure you are playing these correctly and in time. You'll notice that some of these fills have been divided into groups of twos, threes, and fours. This will help you when learning these new fills. Start very slowly at first, and increase the tempo as they become more comfortable.

Chapter 14: Specialty Grooves

Punk Rock Grooves

Punk rock is an anti-establishment rock music genre that emerged in the 1970s. Bands such as the Ramones in New York City, and the Sex Pistols and the Clash in London, were recognized as the pioneers of this new musical movement. In addition to the bands mentioned above, great drummers such as Bill Stevenson from the Descendents/Black Flag/All, Travis Barker from Blink 182,

and Tré Cool of Green Day use the beats provided on this page to drive this very cool style of music. Due to the fast tempos, quarter notes are generally used on the cymbal to keep time. Start slowly and eventually speed up to 200–250+ beats per minute. On the recording, the examples are repeated four times.

Blast Beats

Blast beats are very fast, powerful, heavy, and driving grooves. They were made popular in early hardcore and punk music and can be heard today in the music of bands such as Lamb of God, Strapping Young Lad, Death, Arch Enemy, Slipknot, and Cannibal Corpse.

Start very slowly to ensure your alignment is correct and then start speeding them up to 140–200 bpm.

Traditional Blasts

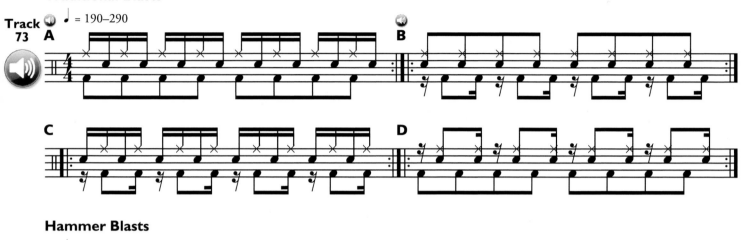

Hammer Blasts

Hammer Blast with Double Bass

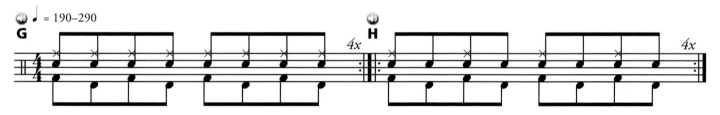

Bomb Blasts

Triplet Blasts

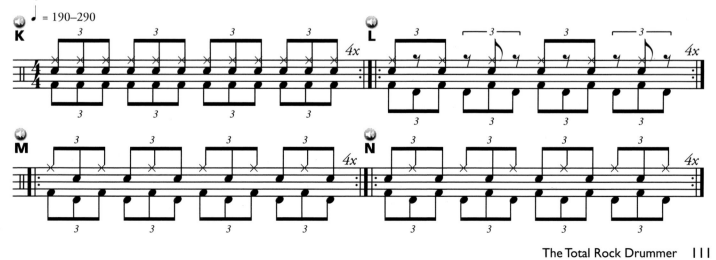

Train Beats

Train beats imitate the sound of a train rolling down the tracks. Play a single-stroke roll on the snare drum to create this effect. There are a few various accented patterns for you to practice. These beats are generally heard in country rock but can also be heard on such popular hits as "Train Time" by Cream, "Lay Down Sally" by Eric Clapton, "Folsom Prison Blues" by Johnny Cash, "On the Road Again" by Willie Nelson, "Yakety Yak" by the Coasters, and "Ballroom Blitz" by Sweet.

Common Snare Patterns with Accents

Common Foot Patterns

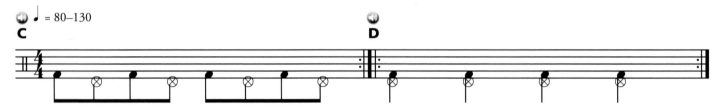

Common Train Beats (Hands and Feet Combined)

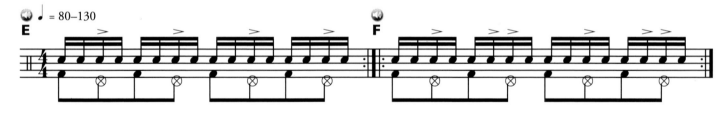

Accent Variations

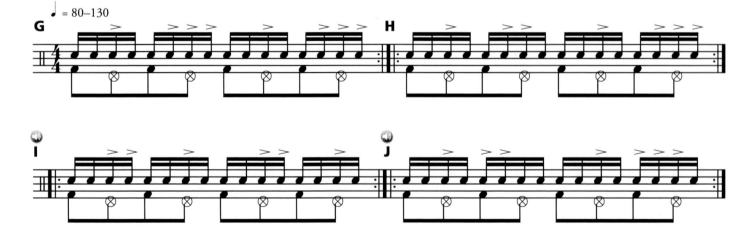

The Bo Diddley Beat

Here's a great groove that you're going to love to play. Guitarist Bo Diddley (1928–2008) was a key figure in the transition from blues to rock 'n' roll. He made this beat very popular in the 1950s with songs like "Hey Bo Diddley" and "Who Do You Love." Variations of the Bo Diddley beat can be heard in "Willie and the Hand Jive" by Johnny Otis, "I Want Candy" by the Strangeloves, and "Desire" by U2.

The Bo Diddley beat is similar to the *3:2 son clave,* a Latin rhythm with three beats in the first half of the bar and two beats in the second half of the bar.

Common Foot Pattern

Floor Tom and Snare

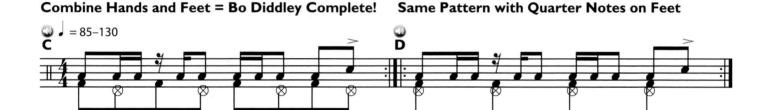

Combine Hands and Feet = Bo Diddley Complete!

Same Pattern with Quarter Notes on Feet

Imply the 3:2 Son Clave on the Bass Drum

Add the Hi-Hat Foot on the "Ands"

Hi-Hat, Bass, and Snare Bo Diddley Groove

Same Pattern with 3:2 Clave in the Bass Drum

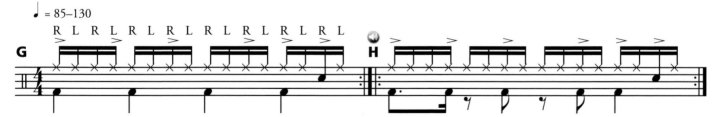

Left Foot 3:2 Son Clave

Left Foot 3:2 Son Clave, Bass Drum on Quarters

Reggae Grooves

Reggae is a highly-rhythmic Jamaican musical form that has become popular all around the world. Reggae grooves can be played straight with an eighth- or sixteenth-note feel, or they can be swung with a triplet feel, depending on the song. These grooves can be challenging at first because many of them have no bass drum on beat 1. Common places for the bass drum to be played are on beats 2 and 4, or only on beat 3. Some reggae grooves will have the bass drum on all four quarter notes, as you'll see in the exercises below.

You'll hear reggae grooves in the music of bands such as Bob Marley, Inner Circle, and King Tubby, and reggae has also influenced rock bands such as the Police, as shown on tracks such as "Walking on the Moon" or "Message in a Bottle."

The following examples use a triplet swing feel. Examples A–D demonstrate the "one drop" reggae groove. "One drop" means you are "dropping," or moving, the bass drum "pulse" from beat 1 to beat 3.

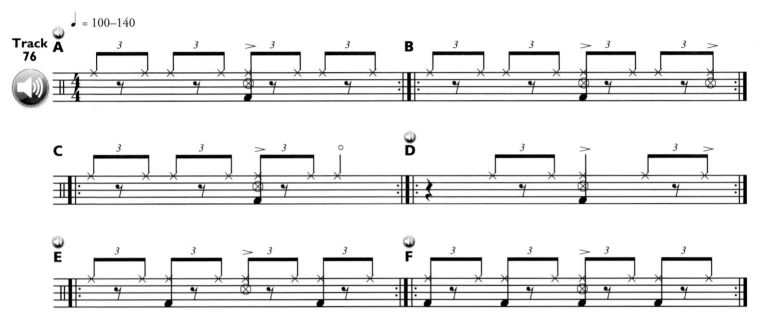

Here are some reggae beats using straight eighth notes and sixteenth notes.

Jungle/Drum 'n' Bass Grooves

Jungle, also known as *drum 'n' bass,* is a newer style of music that is exciting, rhythmic, high-energy, and fast-paced. A lot of drum 'n' bass music is electronic-based, using synthesizers, sequencers, bass, and electronic drums. Drummers such as Steve Smith, Jojo Mayer, and Johnny Rabb are making this great style more recognizable to modern drummers. For more good examples of drum 'n' bass music, check out such artists as Paradox, Aphex Twin, Squarepusher, Verbal Kint, Makato, and more. The goal is to play these grooves at 180bpm or faster. Have fun!

One-Measure Patterns

Two-Measure Patterns

Two-Measure Double-Bass Jungle Grooves

$\quad \quad$ ♩ = 140–200

Track 80

A

B

C

D

E

F

G

Famous Rock Grooves

This section features a collection of classic drum grooves from famous rock drummers. The more songs you know, the more you'll get hired! Have fun with these!

Chad Smith, Red Hot Chili Peppers

"Californication"—Main Groove

Track 81

Alex Van Halen, Van Halen

"Hot for Teacher"—Main Groove After Intro

Track 82

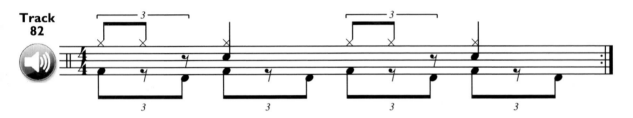

Alex Van Halen (b. 1953), along with his brother, guitarist Eddie, formed Van Halen, one of the most popular rock groups of all time, in the 1970s. Alex is known for his signature sound and his large, multi-tom drumset.

PHOTO COURTESY OF STAR FILE PHOTO, INC.

Stewart Copeland, The Police

"Spirits in the Material World"—Opening Fill into Main Groove

"Message in a Bottle"—Cross-Stick Part in 2nd Chorus

"Walking on the Moon"—Main Groove (Two Measures Before Vocals Start)

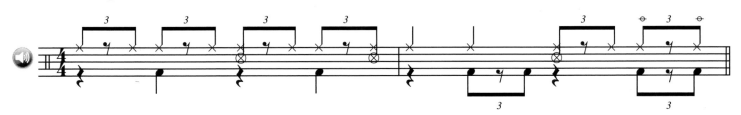

Stewart Copeland (b. 1952) is best known as the drummer for the Police. He was also a member of two "supergroups"— Animal Logic (with Stanley Clarke and Deborah Holland) and Oysterhead (with Les Claypool and Trey Anastasio)—and made guest appearances with many other artists. A well-rounded musician, Copeland has composed musical scores for numerous films and television shows. His drumming is crisp and precise, with strong reggae and jazz influences. Copeland is a master of intricate hi-hat patterns, syncopated rhythms, and tasteful fills that always support the song.

John Bonham, Led Zeppelin

"The Ocean"—Intro Groove

"The Immigrant Song"—Main Groove

"Whole Lotta Love"—Main Groove

John Bonham (1948–1980) was the drummer for Led Zeppelin from the time the band was formed in 1968 until his death in 1980. His innovative recordings with Led Zeppelin continue to influence drummers today.

John Dolmayan, System of a Down

"Chop Suey"—Main Opening Tom Groove

Manu Katche, Robbie Robertson

"Somewhere Down the Crazy River"—Main Groove, Snares Off

Ringo Starr, The Beatles

"Come Together"—Opening Groove

Ringo Starr (b. 1940 as Richard Starkey) first achieved fame as the drummer (and, occasionally, vocalist) for the Beatles. While he was never regarded as a virtuoso soloist during his time with the Beatles, his drum parts were rock-solid and always right for the song. He was also one of the first rock drummers whose personality was an equal ingredient in the group—not an easy task when your bandmates are named Lennon, McCartney, and Harrison! Post-Beatles, Starr embarked on a successful solo career, as well as performing and recording with many other musicians, including solo projects by all three of the former Beatles. He continues to tour with his All-Starr Band, comprised of a revolving group of outstanding musicians.

Lars Ulrich, Metallica

"Master of Puppets"—Four-Bar Main Groove

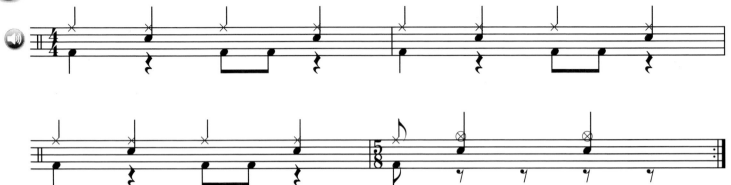

"One"—Main Double-Bass Groove

Lars Ulrich (b. 1963), drummer for the band Metallica since the 1980s, is known for fast and furious double-bass drumming and high-energy performances.

Clive Burr, Iron Maiden

"Run to the Hills"—Intro

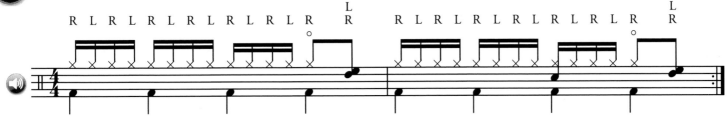

"Run to the Hills"—Chorus

Nicko McBrain, Iron Maiden

"Ghost of the Navigator"—Verse, Main Groove

"Ghost of the Navigator"—End of First Verse/Pre-Chorus

"Subdivisions"—Two-Handed Riding Groove During Intro

"Tom Sawyer"—$\frac{7}{8}$ Groove During Keyboard Melody

"La Villa Strangiato"—Main $\frac{4}{4}$ Groove

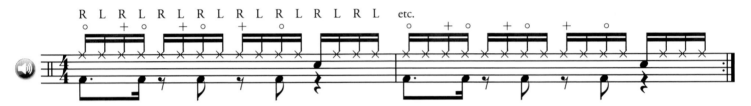

"La Villa Strangiato"—Mellow Middle Linear Section in $\frac{7}{8}$

Neil Peart (b. 1952) is the drummer and lyricist for the Canadian rock trio Rush, an immensely popular group since the mid-1970s. His flawless technique and fluency in playing in unusual time signatures are two of the elements that give the group its characteristic sound.

Danny Carey, Tool

"Schism"—Main Four-Bar Groove, Snares Off

Track 91

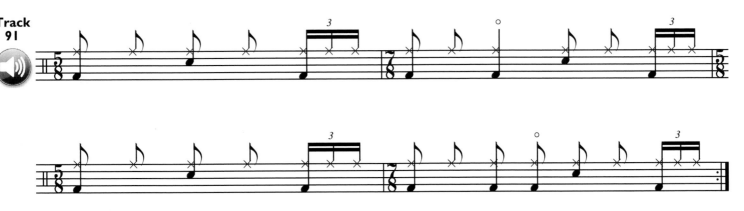

Steve Gadd, Paul Simon

"50 Ways to Leave Your Lover"—Main Groove

Track 92

PHOTO BY DAVID SELIG/COURTESY OF STAR FILE PHOTO, INC.

Steve Gadd (b. 1945) is arguably the greatest session drummer of his generation, appearing on over 600 albums by Paul Simon, Steely Dan, Eric Clapton, Chick Corea, Chuck Mangione, Al Di Meola, and many others. He is highly respected in musical circles for his versatility, near-perfect groove, and dedication to his craft. Gadd has introduced many new rhythms to the pop music genre, such as the Mozambique rhythm in Paul Simon's "Late in the Evening." He is still in demand as a sideman to the top acts in music.

Matt Cameron, Soundgarden

"Jesus Christ Pose"—Main Groove, Vocal Section

Track 93

Tré Cool, Green Day

"Basketcase"—Fill Leading into 2nd Verse

Track 94

Tré Cool (b. 1972 as Frank Edwin Wright III) is the drummer for the pop/punk band Green Day. He lived every musician's dream, watching his high school band grow into a huge commercial success that helped re-define an entire genre. Their major-label debut, Dookie, is a classic in the pop/punk genre. Green Day has sold over 65 million albums, won three Grammy awards, and continue to evolve musically.

Conclusion

This concludes the *Total Rock Drummer*. If you've made it this far, you should have the skills and musical vocabulary to become a successful rock drummer.

One thing that's clear is that rock drumming is a diverse and varied art form. There is no one style, sound, or approach that is "the best." Rather, if you look at the great rock drummers, one thing they all have in common is that they found a good musical "fit" between their drumming and the sound of their bands. The definition of a "good drummer" may vary from one band to the next. By studying as wide a range of rock drumming as possible, you will have a large "tool kit" of beats and fills to draw upon in any given situation.

Above all, keep practicing and listening. Strive to be open-minded and to incorporate all sorts of influences into your rock drumming.

Appendix: Recommended Listening

Artist	Album	Drummer
AC/DC	Any	Phil Rudd
The Beatles	Any	Ringo Starr
Black Sabbath	Paranoid	Bill Ward
Black Sabbath	Master of Reality	Bill Ward
Cream	Any	Ginger Baker
Dream Theater	Any	Mike Portnoy
Genesis	Any	Phil Collins/Chester Thompson
Iron Maiden	Powerslave	Nicko McBrain
Iron Maiden	Number of the Beast	Clive Burr
King Crimson	In the Court of the Crimson King	Michael Giles
King Crimson	Discipline	Bill Bruford
King Crimson	Red	Bill Bruford
Led Zeppelin	Any	John Bonham
Metallica	Ride the Lightning	Lars Ulrich
Metallica	Master of Puppets	Lars Ulrich
Metallica	...And Justice for All	Lars Ulrich
Nirvana	Any	Dave Grohl
Ozzy Osbourne	Bark at the Moon	Tommy Aldridge
Ozzy Osbourne	Blizzard of Ozz	Lee Kerslake
Pink Floyd	Dark Side of the Moon	Nick Mason
Pink Floyd	The Wall	Nick Mason
The Police	Any	Stewart Copeland
The Rolling Stones	Any	Charlie Watts
Rush	Fly By Night	Neil Peart
Rush	Caress of Steel	Neil Peart
Rush	2112	Neil Peart
Rush	Farewell to Kings	Neil Peart
Rush	Hemispheres	Neil Peart
Rush	Permanent Waves	Neil Peart
Rush	Moving Pictures	Neil Peart
Rush	Exit Stage Left	Neil Peart
System of a Down	Any	John Dolmayan
Tool	Any	Danny Carey
Van Halen	1984	Alex Van Halen
The Who	Any	Keith Moon
Yes	Any	Bill Bruford/Alan White